MILLENNIAL MAXIMS

Big Ray

Big Ray Books LLC

ISBN-13: 9798686062214

Cover design by: Big Ray
Library of Congress Control Number: 2018675309
Printed in the United States of America

For my family, my friends, and my enemies.

The fool doth think he is wise, but the wise man knows himself to be a fool.

WILLIAM SHAKESPEARE, "AS YOU LIKE IT"

CONTENTS

MILLENNIAL MAXIMS

OPENING REMARKS

It's well known that a picture is worth a thousand words. But how much is a saying worth, particularly ones like above?

It's definitely worth something. For one it's witty. And it's definitely got a kernel of truth to it. But are sayings like the last one, maxims to be exact, more like fortune cookies or more like encapsulated wisdom? Are they worth discarding after reading or chiseling into the edifice of our mind forever?

I believe, very much, in fact, in the latter. I believe maxims are like small nuggets of gold in the riverbed. I believe they are valuable. And their small size and simple nature makes them worth more than a thousand words, or even a hundred thousand. After all, what can be said quickly is said well, and what is said well can be understood by all. I have nothing against esoteric learning or monographic manuscripts, but there really is nothing I love more than a good turn of phrase, a good saying, or a great maxim!!!

History

As long as there have been spoken words, there must have been short sayings. At first wisdom was simple. The mechanics of nature in its simplest forms.

Perhaps, the great hunter chieftains mused to their young, "To hunt well is to hunt quietly." In any case, it's fair to say maxims have been with humans a long time.

And there have been many a great philosopher who was a great aphorist. Indeed, many a great individual is known for their witty observations: Plato, Napoleon, Jesus, the Buddha, Cervantes, Shakespeare, Benjamin Franklin, Mark Twain, and on and on...

Well, here are a few to wet your beak and prove the power and persistence of the pithy:

"Necessity is the mother of invention."

-Plato

"If you want a thing done well, do it yourself."

-Napoleon Bonaparte

"Take therefore no thought for the morrow: for the morrow shall take thought for the things of itself. Sufficient unto the day is the evil thereof."

-Jesus

"Three things cannot be long hidden: the sun, the moon, and the truth."

-Buddha

"Time ripens all things; no man is born wise."

-Miguel de Cervantes

"Well done is better than well said."

-Benjamin Franklin

"Brevity is the soul of wit."

-William Shakespeare

"If you don't read the newspaper, you're uninformed. If you read the newspaper, you're misinformed."

-Mark Twain

And for those looking for a helping breeze in rough seas:

"Success is not final; failure is not fatal: It is the courage to continue that counts."

-Winston Churchill

Usefulness in the Modern World?

In a world with so much information. The simple. The elegant. The concise is more valuable than ever. And concise wisdom is perhaps the most valuable commodity of all. This book may not be long. It may not be dense. And it may not be about any one thing in particular. But it was my hope this book be useful to a modern audience on the go, ***a tl;dr version of wisdom*** I've accumulated over the years.

Conclusion

What follows is a book of original maxims, aphorisms,

very short stories, poems, puns, and so on. Almost all of the sayings are my own creation, a few I stole, and others I modified. It is the work of a Millennial, and for that reason the book is called *Millennial Maxims*. In some ways the book caters to the Millennial and Gen Z cohorts. However, I hope this book can touch people of all shapes and sizes, ages, and attitudes, because this is a book of wisdom. Now! Please enjoy the book and feel free to bounce from topic to topic!

CHAPTER 1 - NATURE

Nature is beyond words.

Nature is fractal.

Nature is infinite and limited.

Nature is beyond logic and yet logic can make some sense of it.

If you want to understand nature, then go spend time in it. If you really want to understand nature, then go live in it. If you really, really want to understand nature, then never leave it, and make your living off of it.

A stroll through nature is cheaper than talk-therapy and more effective.

If it weren't for Central Park, all the people in Manhattan would go mad.

If you're looking for clarity, there is no better place to go than the woods, the beach, the mountains, the desert, nature, nature, nature is the clearest place there is. No confusion among the trees, in the hills, within the mountains, through the canyons, on the rivers, or anywhere in nature because nature knows what it is, where its been, and where its going. If you can tap into that, you can tap into your own clarity.

Nature is brutal. Nature is beautiful. Nature is hell. Nature is heaven. Nature is winner take all. Nature is here for all. Nature is whatever you make it.

If you have a question, seek your answer in nature.

Nature is great for snapping you out of your psychological nonsense.

Nature is great for snapping you into existential God sense.

Nature is great for snapping you in two.

People often flee the city for the forest, but hardly ever the forest for the city.

If a city is about greed, ambition, jealousy, nature is about oneness, humility, and appreciation.

Growing up in the country makes a kid healthy, wealthy, and wise.

If a child spends its first 10 years in nature, their imagination will blossom like a field of flowers, their courage will swell like a river after a flood, and their love of life will grow like a great redwood!!!

A famous author once said, "A design is perfected when there is nothing left to take away." There is nothing left to take away when it comes to nature.

If you're looking for inspiration, a solution, a burst of creativity, take a walk in the woods, a swim in the ocean, or a hike up a mountain.

Nature lets you know that when you're gone the world won't even miss a beat. In other words, your problems are not worth the worry.

All life's lessons are in nature.

There is no greater grounding effect than walking barefoot in nature.

If you're ill, spending time in a clean flowing river, can work wonders.

If you're looking for enlightenment, there's no better place to look than under a tree. At the very least you'd be in good company. Just take a seat and meditate.

If you can deal with the wilderness, you can deal with anything.

An education by books is good, by family is great, by nature is best.

When you learn to breathe like a tree, slow and steady, even in the storm, then you'll achieve just about anything you want.

When you learn to see like a snake, deep and penetrating, even at night, then your timing will be impeccable professionally and personally.

When you learn to smell like a dog, discerning and deciphering, even in a crowd, then your first impressions will be spot on.

When you learn to move like a cat, fast and gracefully, even from repose, then you'll win in games of strength and skill.

When you learn to remember like an elephant, then you'll work will be original and your contributions useful.

When you learn to eat like a lion, then you'll stop being fat and start being lean.

When you learn to eat like a gorilla, then you'll be both strong and flexible.

When you learn to flow like a river, then your actions will produce results and your attitude will be well-suited to whatever situations you find yourself in.

When you learn to stand like a mountain, then your goals will be achieved no matter the whims and weathers, no matter the slings and arrows, no matter anything.

CHAPTER 2 - SPORTS

In sports, good mechanics makes you look like a magician.

All sports are far more mental than we care to admit.

The most mental of all sports is golf. Tennis is second. And Baseball is third. Why you ask? The pauses. The length of time between the action. In the above three, the action is short lived, and the inaction is long lived. In basketball, football, and football (soccer) the action is continuous, fast-paced, and requires instinct more than conscious thought.

Tennis is a great way to watch the battle of two individual wills. Basketball is a great way to watch the battle of two team wills. And golf is a great way to watch the battle of one will against itself, nature, and an impossible game.

A child that does not engage in sport early on, will struggle to engage with life later on.

The joy of sports is immediate feedback, good or bad, at least you know where you stand. So often in modern life, the payoff is years away.

Frequent participation in sports is the surest cure I know for the ills and worries of our techno-addicted way of being.

Continuous improvement in a sport brings hope to other facets of life.

Sport is humbling, and that's good if your ego has swelled due to success in the material world.

If you want to impress young girls, nothing does the trick better than prowess in sports.

If you want to reach the professional ranks of any sport the recipe is simple: start young, play often, and be luckier than a lottery winner.

If you want to improve rapidly at any sport, apply the 80/20 principle. Find the 20% of techniques or actions that create 80% of the value in the game. In tennis, you'll want to focus on your serve, your forehand, and your footwork. In golf, you'll want to focus on the fundamentals: grip, stance, backswing, downswing, and ball position. In basketball: focus on proper passing, dribbling, and proper shooting technique. In weightlifting: focus on proper technique for the squat, dead-lift, and bench press. In any sport, really, just focus on the most used techniques, and save the fancy stuff for later. At first you just want to get going, get enjoyment, and get competing with people without holding play up.

Aside from 80/20, the best way to improve at a sport, and the worst thing for your ego, is…drum roll please…Play Against People Better than You!

Getting to the top of any pyramid is difficult, getting to the top of a sports pyramid is insanely difficult.

The reason I think sporting greats are worthy of admiration is this: they've managed to unify their mind, body, and spirit in an intense way, a conscious way, to make their own way.

The reason I think sporting greats are unworthy of admiration is this: they've pissed away talent, pissed on their fans, and generally been pissed off despite having a gift from God so few have and so many want.

All great yogis have great presence, gathered through years, even lifetimes of meditation and spiritual practice. But the closest an ordinary man or woman can get to total presence is sports. That is truly their value. They teach the beauty and absolute necessity of total involvement because you can't hit a 90-mph fastball while thinking about what you have to do tomorrow.

There's no comeback like a sports comeback.

Choking is a real thing in life. Sports just makes it obvious.

Success in sports feels the sweetest and failure in sports tastes the most bitter.

Gambling on sports is often more fun the playing in them.

To be great at sports you either have to be really dumb or really smart.

In 50 years, the NFL will be a shadow of its former self.

Sports commentators come in two flavors: deliciously good or dismally bland.

Sports are the ultimate meritocracy, and thus the least merciful profession on earth. And therefore, the most impossible calling for most people.

Deep in every red-blooded man's heart is the desire to be a famous, well-paid, and good-looking professional athlete. Why is this so? Because despite all modern appearances, man is a hunter, a killer, and a conqueror. And except for the military, sport is the only high-status place left on this planet for a hunter, a killer, and a conqueror to seek glory. (business success is too abstract for most)

CHAPTER 3 - SEX

Sex can either be divine or disgusting. The determination is up to you.

Sex is two becoming one in order to have fun.

If sex didn't feel so good, the world would be a much duller place.

Paying for sex may scratch the itch, but it can leave one feeling like a bitch.

When two people have sex, they exchange a lot more than fluids.

A famous author once hinted that sex is much ado about nothing. She may have been right. But without sex there would be nothing.

Seduction is the art of getting sex.

Sex is like success in this life, short-lived and in short supply for most people.

There's no greater regret than the regret of passing up great sex with a great person on a great night.

There are a few things you don't need to be good at to enjoy. Sex is one of them.

Having Tinder sex is like getting fast food after midnight, delightful in the moment, regretful in the morning.

I've been told there's nothing like sex on LSD, except of course sex on LSD and mushrooms.

When you're having sex on a regular basis you wonder what the big deal is?

Everyone can say unprotected sex is a stupid idea in hindsight, but in the sight of the moment it's probably the greatest thing since sliced bread.

Every woman a man looks at for more than 10 seconds he would like to sleep with. But the world is a cruel place. And most men have probably slept with less than 1% of 1% of all the women they've ever truly desired.

Women may lust over a man's wallet. But men lust over a women's everything. From head to toe, there's nothing in a woman that doesn't inspire absolute lust in a man.

I once met a man who had sex with over 100 hundred women in Tijuana, I asked what he learnt, he said, "How not to get an STD."

There are three things driving everything on this planet for just about everyone: eating, sleeping, and sex. Of the three, sleeping moves the world the least. Eating moves the world a little more. And sex moves the world like an engine moves a car, totally!

Men are willing to suffer a million slights, a million fights, a million blights, just to get a bite of a woman.

Men may move mountains, they may build businesses, they may invent endless gadgets, they may conquer endless countries, they may write endless ballads, they may do any number of amazing things, but were it not for sex, not for women, men would still be in a cave poking a fire and getting high off native fungi.

Women are willing to spend hours on their makeup, days on their wardrobe, months on their physique, just to reel in the right man.

Women may put on so many airs, airs of mystery, airs of indifference, airs of aloofness, airs of busyness, airs of betterment, airs of success, airs of cosmopolitaness, airs of travel, airs of intelligence, airs of grace, airs of good judgement, airs of good taste, but were it not for sex, not for men, they would all walk around pale face, fat bottomed, and in total ignorance to world affairs.

Back in the day, women lured men in with sex, but they kept them with their cooking. Today, women lure men in with sex, and keep them with it too.

Getting sex is a flex.

Sex is the ultimate blackmail tool.

Sex is why the internet took off.

In todays workplace, sex has destroyed more careers than it has advanced.

Despite its' absolute necessity, lack of physical complexity, and all-around brevity, sex is still the most taboo entity.

Sex, sex, sex, you can get it with an amex, sex, sex, sex, no one likes with latex.

CHAPTER 4 - RELATIONSHIPS

If your relationships feel like business arrangements, they're not any fun. If they feel like soap operas, they're too much fun. Right in the middle is where you want the feeling.

I once saw an elderly couple sitting in the grass drinking hard seltzer, they took hearty sips, laughed often, and only looked at their phones to decline a call. This is the simplicity of love.

It's been well observed that the game of love is the most joyous and cruelest of all games. But it's a game we all must play. At one time or another. Even nuns are in love with Jesus. Although perhaps, that one is a little like unrequited love.

A dog is in love with his bone. A man is in love with his woman. And a yogi is in love with the universe.

A good country love song can teach you as much about love and relationships as any book.

If you're lucky, your sexual relations are one to many. If you're unlucky, they're one to none. If your picky, they're one to one.

Simps are wannabe pimps.

Most divorces nowadays happen because of Disney. Everyone expects a fairytale. But gets a hairytale.

I've known some women that can't stand being alone. And I've known some men that are more than willing to spend a night with a stranger. But I've never met a stranger named Ranger who only looked for Danger.

Most people assume you end up marrying your mother or father when you find your spouse. But that's only partially true.

Long lasting intimate relationships are like your favorite dish from your favorite restaurant.

A relationship that doesn't grow doesn't go.

Keeping a relationship healthy is like tending to a garden. You have to create the right atmosphere. Water. Soil. Sun. Before anything good can emerge.

Human beings and dolphins are the only mammals that have sex for fun. But only human beings make a big deal about it.

Most millennials get into relationships thru a mobile app. I guess the nerds win after all.

The most important relationship is not with anyone.

When you say the word relationship most people think

about sex. But what they should think about is everything.

Fat people in America have a really good relationship with large corporations that provide them with delicious, highly processed, scientifically engineered poison.

Most people love dogs because they are the only relationship that is unconditional. Every other is strings attached.

How you relate to your phone nowadays says a lot about you.

In America, a healthy relationship with drugs get you into the corner office. An unhealthy relationship puts you on the corner.

Relationships are all about give and take. Though, you give too much, and you get your guy or gal taken away. And if you give too little, then your guy or gal gives themselves a way to another. It's: A catch twenty-two. A tightrope. A tango on a cliff. And when you make it work it seems like God himself is smiling down on you.

Most relationships are like the seasons, sometimes hot, sometimes cold, but they should never get old.

Good relationships start with communication, and bad one's end without it.

Most relationships start with a bang and end with a whimper.

Most marriages today are a match made in hell.

Long marriages are a match made in money.

Short marriages are a match made in misery.

If you want a relationship to last, don't dwell on the past, and just remember it all goes by too fast.

A great relationship is like a great soup, different ingredients combined well.

CHAPTER 5 - MONEY

Some people say money is the root of all evil. But that's just an excuse. At the end of the day, people are the root of all evil.

It's a well-known truism that money makes the world go round. But it's wrong, the world goes round all on its own. Money just makes people go round and round.

When you have money, it's the thing that matters least to you. When you don't have money, it's the thing that matters most to you. When you have just enough money, you're afraid of losing what you got and dead set on getting more while you can.

Everything costs money, but the things you really want can't be bought.

If you have enough money, the world is your oyster.

Those born into money have an altogether different hell to pull themselves out of than those born without it.

Once you get a taste for money and the power it brings, your appetite only grows like a fat man eating his first course at a Michelin starred restaurant.

Many people are interested in manifesting money in

their lives, they'll do all manner of rituals, rites, and practices; of course, they neglect the most important principle, to get more gold you have to be golden and golden people follow the golden rule. In other words, you will be a money magnet when you offer value to others.

Some people are so identified with their money that when they lose it, they give up on life.

The few people who win the lottery lose something far greater.

To accumulate an ungodly amount of money you need a lot of perspiration, perseverance, and divine provenance, in other words you need to work your ass off, work thru failure, and work the wheel of fortune. The first two you can control, the last you cannot. Therefore, always work on the formers and leave the last to the past.

Based on observation, it seems the ways to become a billionaire are thusly: 1) be born into a family of billions, 2) found an innovative company, take it public, and cash out your stock options upon substantial appreciation; alternatively, keep it private, and grow it over decades with good ole fashioned elbow grease, 3) be the best athlete in a mainstream sport (basketball, football, golf, etc.), 4) learn the art of high finance, found a hedge fund, predict a market crash, collect the gains, 5) stage a military coup of a resource rich country, install yourself as the unquestioned leader of the country, invite multinational energy extractors, collect the tax on the extraction, watch out for assassination from your ministers and generals. These are the ways to become a billionaire. Good luck!

Based on observation, it seems the ways to become a millionaire are more varied than the aforementioned and are thusly: 1) start a fast food restaurant, expand to many locations, collect positive cash flows for many years, reinvest in the business, enjoy your moderate wealth, 2) write a series of best-selling books, 3) play a professional sport at the highest level, 4) become a doctor at a preeminent medical center or hospital, 5) become a lawyer at a preeminent law firm or corporation, 6) become a software engineer at a prominent technology company, 7) start a retail chain, expand to many locations, collect positive cash flows for many years, reinvest in the business, enjoy your moderate wealth, 8) start an auto dealership business, expand to many locations, etc. 9) become world class at poker, 10) start a brewery, expand to many locations, etc. 11) invent a new device or manufacturing process, patent it, collect the royalties, 12) rob a bank or armored car, 13) sell high margin drug products like cocaine, 14) start an oil drilling company, strike oil, collect the positive cash flow quickly, close your operation once the price of oil drops, enjoy your moderate wealth, 15) start an ecommerce company based on lifestyle branding, expand thru social media advertising, go viral, update the catalog with fresh products, enjoy your moderate wealth, 16) develop fun and useful mobile applications, advertise the hell out of them, collect the positive cash flows, invest in more apps, enjoy your moderate wealth, 17) win a Nobel prize, 18) win a Fields medal, 19) win a minor regional lottery, 20) take out a life insurance policy on yourself, fake your death, collect the money thru intermediaries, enjoy your moderate wealth in moderate seclusion, 21) work a moderate wage job for many hours, save and be tighter with your money than a company in bankruptcy, enjoy your moderate wealth deep into your middle ages, 22) rise up the ranks of a corporation, get a corner office, negotiate for stock options, cash them out when the stock price booms, 23) marry a rich man or woman, 24) more generally, start any kind of business, expand it, sell it to someone, enjoy your moderate wealth, 25) alternatively, start any kind of business, expand it, take profits, enjoy your moderate wealth, 26) inherit it from a rich aunt or uncle, 27) buy cheap land, wait for developers, sell to the highest bidder, 28) work hard for a time, take all your money to Vegas, play poker or blackjack until you hit it big, enjoy your moderate wealth, 29) work hard for a time, put all your money in the stock market, predict a market collapse, hit it big and take profits, enjoy your moderate wealth, 30) collect random memorabilia, sell it once a market develops, enjoy your moderate wealth, 31) become a crooked politician, 32) become a famous actor, 33) become a world renowned Guru. These are the ways, in my humble estimation to become a millionaire. (Sidebar, if you want to be poor, do none of the above.)

For men, it's not that money buys them happiness, it's that money buys you women, and women make men happy, especially when they're drop dead gorgeous.

For women, it's not that money buys them happiness, it's that money buys them overpriced luxury status goods that boost their self-esteem in relation to other women.

Poor people hate the rich because they have money. Rich people hate the poor because they don't have money. And the middle class gets screwed. It's a great system until it's not.

A sure sign of the noveau rich is the latest and greatest, gadgets, clothes, and accessories.

A sure sign of the landed aristocracy is subtlety and indifference alongside an absolute opulent estate with horses.

Most people spend the greater part of their lives chasing money only to find they didn't need much to be happy after all.

Some people spend the greater part of their lives chasing money only to find they wish they had more.

In America, the more money you have, the more you matter, and the more you matter the better you're supposed to feel.

Most people would be surprised to hear that the paper money they spend is created out of thin air by a private corporation masquerading as a government entity immune from Federal laws constructed under false pretenses by European banking dynasties in the most shadowy of settings. But then again most people are mostly stupid. After all, intelligence is a bell curve, and because of a little thing called mathematics, precisely half the population is below the average. It's too bad they're not a little smarter because if they were, they may just get upset and start a revolution.

Before money people bartered, after money they will barter again, but first we must use Bitcoin!

Money ain't what it used to be. Our grandparents could buy an awful lot more with a dollar. Now even the dollar menu at McDonalds is gonna cost you a few bones.

There are a few ways to get money. And a million ways to lose it.

I've heard some great men say, "Money is just a way to keep score." If that's the case, what's the game?

Some of the worst real estate deals ever made were done by Native Americans. You see, they had no concept of money, no need for it, no history of it. So, when the Europeans came, they couldn't help themselves. A few blankets for the Ohio River Valley, a few seashells for Manhattan, and so on. I don't think greater real estate deals will ever occur on this green earth. But who knows, maybe there are some Martians we can bamboozle once Elon Musk gets to Mars.

Most of your taxes go to paying down the debt owed to the Federal Reserve. The rest goes to the military. And the rest of what's left go to unfunded liabilities, like Social Security and Medicare, and not to mention the leviathan itself, the administration of the Federal Government. Don't worry, though, the crumbs that go to your kids' education, this country's infrastructure, and healthcare are plenty to go around, just look around, and you can see.

The best thing money can buy you isn't happiness, it's a country club membership inside a gated community. And if you've never been, you should go and see. There are no upside-down smiles inside country club lane.

If you're too frugal with money you never enjoy it. If you're too loose with money you never keep it. If you don't give a damn about money you never lose it.

People that brag about how much money they have are poor souls indeed.

When you come into a great deal of money, resist the temptation to tell everyone you know about it, trust me. Unless of course, you want to be pitched more cockamamie business ideas than Mark Cuban, Mr. Wonderful, Daymond Green, and Lorie Grenier on Shark Tank. Then, by all means shout it from the hilltops.

The best things to do with your money in descending order: Invest it, Save it, Spend it.

If you want to be well-paid be better than everyone else. And being better simply means being able to do things they can't do, being able to do things they can do but faster and being able to learn things they can't.

Jesus Christ expounded upon the golden rule, namely, Do unto Others as You want done unto yourself. Capitalists also expounded upon the golden rule, namely, He who has the Gold makes the Rules. Who was right?

Money can make a happy person ecstatic, but it can't make a depressed person euphoric.

The more wisdom you have the less money matters. The more money you have the less wisdom matters. The more wisdom and money you have the more good you will do for others and not yourself.

The latest and greatest money scheme today is the charitable foundation. From Bill and Melinda Gates Foundation to the Clinton foundation. It's clear to see if you want to know, no greater tax-free slush fund has ever been devised. Bravo to the financial engineers, public relations gurus, and 501(c) legal wizards, you've done a great service to the world!

Money is the blood that keeps the economic body moving. If it clogs in certain cliques, you get a market shattering heart attack. If it flows freely throughout, you get health which is the first wealth.

CHAPTER 6 - GAMBLING & LUCK

People don't go to Vegas to get drunk, win big money, or get laid; they go to feel something, they go to experience something, they go because everyday life in America is boring.

The key to gambling on sports according to greats like Billy Walters is this: watch the line, watch the odds, and don't bet with the suckers.

Russian roulette is the only game of chance I don't recommend. All other games I thoroughly endorse. Well, except for slots. They are rigged, don't you know?

Lady Luck is fickler than the weather.

In the future there will be computer applications that let you bet on anything. And I do mean anything. For instance, whether your buddy graduates from college, whether so and so gets pregnant out of wedlock, and even whether someone dies before a certain age. You think social media is bad now, wait till there's no privacy and everyone can bet on anything!

Buying a lottery ticket is the worst kind of gambling. Playing the stock market is much better. But betting on yourself is best.

Peoples. Places. The great wheel of fortune turns for us all, how does it turn for thee?

When the winds of luck are blowing with you, guard against your arrogance. When the winds of luck are blowing against you, guard against your apathy. When the winds of luck neither blow with or against you, take action because you're not moving!!!

Julius Caesar was lucky 99.999% of his life.

Lucky people tend toward ignorance. Unlucky people toward wisdom.

All those who wake with the sun and rest with the moon should count themselves lucky to have gotten thru another day.

The Chinese middle and upper class are world renowned for their pernicious predilections for superstition and gambling.

Would you rather be lucky, good, or from the hood?

People that smoke a pack of cigarettes a day and don't get cancer are both lucky and unlucky.

A beautiful woman was born lucky but thru bad decisions may come into a great deal more bad luck.

If you bet on the underdog the payout is bigger but the probability is smaller. If you bet on the favorite the payout is smaller but the probability is greater. If you're lucky it doesn't matter either way.

If you survive a war, you're lucky.

Risking your life for another is gambling made divine.

Risky behavior either gets rewarded or doesn't, the difference is luck, skill, and weather.

Going All In feels good because you let the Divine Decide.

Never taking a risk is the biggest risk of all.

If you risk it all enough times you're bound to lose.

Losing your luck feels like losing a lover. You don't know if it will ever come back again in one form or another.

Regaining your luck feels like falling in love all over again. You're so glad its back and you never want to lose it again.

For most people, luck ebbs and flows. It comes in streaks. Some last for days. Others for weeks. For a few—years. But in the end, it comes and goes, and it's up to you to knows.

CHAPTER 7 - HEDONISM, PARTYING, AND FUN

Philosophers often decry hedonists for their cavalier cavorting thru life while the latter party. You decide who's having more fun.

The modern embodiment of the god of wine and hedonism, Dionysus/Bacchus, is Dan Bilzerian. It's good to know some things never die. And some ways never shy.

From the poor to the rich, there isn't a great deal of shared sentiment. Though, in my experience, they both love a good party.

The difference between a high-class and a low-class party is the hors d'oeuvres, dress code, and foreplay wordplay.

You know parties are great because even rich snobs enjoy them.

The best fun is free, and the worst fun is for a fee.

How you get your kicks is up to you, at least it should be.

If you want to throw a great party on the cheap do this: make a jungle juice alcoholic party bowl, buy 50 pieces of fried chicken, buy paper plates, tell people to byob (bring your own beer) and byod (bring your own drugs). Sit back and enjoy the mayhem.

The biggest buzzkill for an upper middle-class party is fighting. Please discourage it.

Most men measure the fun of parties by the female to male ratio. A great party is 4 to 1. A good party is 2 to 1. An o.k. party is 1 to 1. Everything below that is a travesty, tragedy, and terror.

There is a sizeable portion of the U.S. population that cannot dance without a few drinks in their blood.

One of the greatest travesties of the modern party is the prevalence and pervasiveness of smartphones. Nothing like walking into a room where everyone has their head down.

If you think you're missing out when your friends are having a party and you're not there, you are, but so are they.

Sometimes the best parties are between partners.

The ideal size for a party is a function of beer per person, square footage, and male to female ratio at or around 50:50.

The worst kinds of parties are with the worst kinds of people.

A party out in the country is a whole other can of worms.

Parties constituted of entirely men ought to have games as their centerpiece. Poker is preferred.

Parties constituted of entirely women ought to have gossip as their centerpiece. Local happenings are preferred.

Parties constituted of men and women ought to have dancing, games, and gossip as their centerpiece. Drinking games, lively music, and local happenings are preferred.

A party filled with psychedelics ought to have positive participants, in a heightened state, negativity will feel ten times worse and some of you might even see it manifested physically. No Bueno!

For a gold digger, the best kind of party is a room filled with rich men.

For a pickup artist, the best kind of party is a room filled with loose and lonely women.

For a writer, the best kind of party is a room filled with lovely young female fans, preferably after a book reading.

For a misanthrope, the best kind of party is an empty room and full bar.

For a billionaire, the best kind of party is a private one filled only with friends and adorable admirers, preferably on ones' own estate.

For a glutton, the best kind of party is a buffet.

For a hedonist, the best kind of party is an orgy filled with drugs and earthly comforts.

For a German, the best kind of party is a Beerfest.

For a Frenchman, the best kind of party is a revolution.

For a Russian, the best kind of party is a vodka filled revolution.

For an Englishman, the best kind of party is a quiet one with whisky, cigars, and snootiness.

For a Spaniard, the best kind of party is a family one with wine and late-night dinners.

For a Korean the best kind of party is a drinking one with barbecue, family and homemade kimchi.

For a Mexican the best kind of party is a drinking kind with a local band, local friends, and local food.

For a Canadian the best kind of party is a cold one with cold beer and cold sports, preferably hockey but curling is acceptable.

For an American the best kind of party is a barbeque filled with beer and football (the rough kind).

The best kind of parties are the spontaneous ones with amazing sunsets in amazing settings with amazing people. In other words, the best kinds of parties are Corona Beer parties. lol. Drink responsibly! Huh? Isn't the point of drinking to be irresponsible? How about this: drink moderately but enjoy excessively. Much better!

CHAPTER 8 - SPIRITUALITY

In America spirituality has become another corporate capitalist media business scam. But then again for the people who commodify everything—is it really any surprise?

The most spiritually advanced country in the world is India. The least spiritually advanced country in the world is Communist China. It used to be the United States, but the Chinese caught up along many fronts, including this one.

True spiritual awakening feels like having been blind and now seeing for the first time.

It's hard to talk about spirituality because it has nothing to do with logic.

They say Zen is not anything that can be talked about or pointed too. But there is a famous story of a Zen Master walking with a pupil. The pupil asks the Master, "What is Zen?" The Master replies, "Do you hear the mountain stream in the distance? That is Zen. The pupil listens, but hears nothing, the question he asked is still bouncing around in his mind, "No, Master I don't hear the stream, but please just tell me what Zen is." The Master said no more and walked on in silence.

Meditation is just a matter of mind. Once you have no mind, it does not matter.

Transcendent experience is, like so many things, a matter of trial and error.

Psychedelic drugs are a portal into the mystical and spiritual, but they are a pale substitute for the real thing based on real effort.

Once you carry your mind, body, and emotions as loosely and freely as your purse or backpack, then you will truly begin to live fully.

Your body, you have gathered. Your mind, you have developed. Your spirit, you have forever.

Spirituality is not about religion. Spirituality is not about ancient texts. Spirituality is not a movement. Spirituality is a reality you must face, discover, and explore from the inside-out.

A malnourished spirit will hold back even the greatest person.

A good spiritual diet incudes meditation, fasting, and time in nature.

Spiritual success will pay dividends in this life and the next. Material success will not.

It's a peculiar feature of human nature that great spiritual awakenings are usually preceded by great accumulated suffering. Not all, but a great many.

There is a realm beyond logic, beyond words, beyond measurement, but not beyond experience...this is the realm of spirituality.

The only thing I can say for certain about spirituality is that it's a word.

Spiritual scams are of the worst kind of scams.

Spiritual experiences are the best kind of experiences.

The great sages and gurus have often been turned into deities and religious figureheads by ambitious and conspiratorial men. But as one great sage once said, "the kingdom of heaven is within." Indeed, look not for signs and wonders, but look within.

CHAPTER 9 - EMOTIONS

Emotions are like the seasons, sometimes gloomy, sometimes glorious, but always changing, never the same.

Steady emotions are the mark of a great man and a noble woman.

Volatile emotions are the mark of a troubled man and a loose woman.

Emotions are just energy in motion.

Life without emotions is like dinner without desert.

If you can master your emotions, then you can surely master your life. But if your emotions are your master, then you will be a slave all your life.

Sweet emotions are a blessing, while bitter emotions are a curse.

Rough seas can lead to rough emotions. Calm seas can lead to smooth emotions.

If you can be happy in your emotions when your surroundings are unhappy then you have mastered the energy within, and your life will be good regardless of the circumstances.

There are as many emotions as there are fruits, so many flavors, so many textures, so many subtleties.

During a full moon, your emotions will come to the surface like a submarine docking in port. Be not alarmed, just observe, and if your great conserve it and put that energy in motion toward your meaning.

Some sports demand great emotion, others demand great stoicism. Some actions are best done with emotion, others not so much. Some people are too emotional, others aren't emotional enough. Some emotions are fun, others are fraught. In some ways our emotions are our lives, in others they are just winds of constant change.

Pain is the deepest emotion for most people, but it's also the most time consuming. Joy is the most time enriching emotion, but it' also the shallowest emotion for most people.

Most human's emotional system is not a lot different than the mouse on the wheel waiting for cheese.

There is nothing like the stock market to bring out the best and worst in male emotions.

There is no emotional blow greater than the loss of a child, except perhaps the loss of a lover.

The wheel of emotions for many is like the wheel of fortune, anyone and anything can spin it and send you flying. Have you ever wanted more stability? More control? More order in your energies?

Emotion is like a heavy rainstorm; it can be a great creative force or a great destructive force. The choice is yours.

Great Actors have an immense reservoir of emotional energy.

You don't want your surgeon to be an "emotional" guy or gal. You do want your artists to be "emotional" guys and gals.

You may or may not like your emotions, but you'll certainly have them.

Having emotions is a little bit like the saying, "better to have loved and lost, then to have never to have loved at all." At least you know you're not dead when you have them.

Blue is to sky as fear is to people.

It's hard to get motivated without emotion. But if you rely solely on emotion it'll be hard to get anything done. As with all things strike a balance.

Fear is a fast track to failure.

Underlying all negative emotion is the fear of death. It is the fear that comes with the knowledge the party will go on without us and we won't have another shot at that guy or gal, another round of beer pong, another chance to network, to laugh, to cry, to make spontaneous plans, to feel anything in the same way again. But it's all so silly when you stop thinking and you start knowing the truth of your existence.

Once you understand how effective food is at fomenting certain emotions, diet becomes deliberate and your destiny is your decision.

A burst of anger is a burst of insanity.

Greed is one emotion people think runs the world, but jealousy is the one emotion that makes the world go round.

Will the architects of artificial intelligence include emotion in their creations? And if not, will the masters of tomorrow be worse than the masters of today?

How far you go in this life is largely a function of how effective your emotions are.

Thoughts and emotions are like two dancers doing the tango, how well they follow the music is how much fun they create.

Greed is an emotion that is healthy until it's not. Love is an emotion that is beautiful until its lust. And every emotion, just like every particle has its anti-particle, has its opposite, but opposite in degree not in design.

The distinguishing emotion for man and animals is desire, desire beyond food, desire beyond reproduction, desire beyond survival, desire for something more, desire for the Ultimate.

FOMO, or the fear of missing out, is the strongest emotion among the young in the world today. In ancient Rome you could only dream how the other half lived, today you can receive second by second updates. The end result is nothing short of discontent squared, jealousy cubed, and anxiety quadrupled.

The antidote to FOMO is and always has been Total Presence in Your Reality, whether it's alone in a room with no one to talk to, with friends you don't really like in a place you don't want to be, or a job you know stinks and you're working to get out of. Don't hate on your life situations, don't hate on yourself. Love your life situations, love yourself, and you'll be amazed how things can change outside once they change on the inside.

CHAPTER 10 – TECHNOLOGY

Technology never went so far than when it brought us the wheel.

Most technology stocks are the tulips of today.

The high-tech monopolies of today are built on electronic bits, the high-tech monopolies of yesterday were built on steel beams. The high-tech monopolies of tomorrow will be built on artificial brains.

The high priests of technology are programmers. And the devout followers are all those glued to their phones.

Modern technology and capitalism tend toward the inhumane, the profane, and often the lame.

Some have speculated that Nikola Tesla's greatest technological feats have yet to surface.

Social media apps have taken off because women want to show themselves off, as is natural and right, and because men want to secure women for themselves, as is natural and right.

Tinder has reduced courtship to a series of high-resolution fictions.

Tinder is a great invention if you're a beautiful lonely girl on a Friday night.

Tinder is a great invention if you're a hungry handsome man on a Friday night.

Tinder is a bad invention if you're an average girl or gal on a Friday night looking for love in the age of temptation.

Facebook started as a DOD-DARPA project called Life-Log. The successful execution of a plan set in motion far in the past is eerie to the say the least.

In the United States there is a close and not too often disclosed romance between the Military and High-Tech companies, this even includes those virtue signaling Silicon Valley Start-Ups.

The reason Silicon Valley is so innovative is because of the great weather, the big blue Pacific Ocean, and the allure of California Girls.

The reason the Midwest is not so innovative is because of the depressing weather, the big yellow fields, and the plainness of the Midwest girls.

The reason Europe is not as innovative as America is because the former has been there done that, the people just want to relax after countless centuries of invention, invasion, and intensity.

The reason America is the most innovative country in the world is because of freedom, envy, and law. These three account for so much of the genius of America.

Elon Musk's companies will succeed because he is implicitly supported by the Military-Industrial Complex of the United States; it also helps that he is a genius.

Many youths will be lost to virtual reality video games in the next fifty years.

Quantum leaps in 3-D manufacturing will usher in a noveau renaissance in craftsmanship. It will be called a Maker Revolution. And the local will finally have a place again in the economy of our lives.

Technology picks no sides. Humans do.

Technology is just an extension of our faculties, our ability to see, to hear, to smell, to taste, to touch. All our technology is just an extension of these. We have not invented anything original, anything new, or anything beyond our physical senses.

The best paying jobs our always in the most high-tech fields. 1000 years ago, that was farming. 100 years ago, that was mechanical and electrical engineering. And today it is in software engineering.

The worst paying jobs are those for which no or little technology is involved. Jobs where human hands reign. It's sad but true.

Technology has given us material comfort and psychological discomfort all at the same time.

Nerds gravitate toward technology because it takes high-powered intellects to solve technical problems.

Technology always creates winners and losers. The more breathtaking the technology, the bigger the winners and the losers. The economic disparity will grow beyond imagination with the advent of Artificial Intelligence.

CHAPTER 11 – MATHEMATICS

Humans may think in words. But God thinks in numbers.

Maths, as the English call it, is the sharpest tool in the shed of human intelligence and the least cultivated among everyday people.

Proving a difficult mathematics proof is the intellectual equivalent of running a marathon.

Mathematical thinking is the most rigorous kind of thinking.

Great creative bridges exist between Mathematics and Art. If you only look, you will find them.

There is a mathematics which underlies everything, we have only to uncover it, and we can be masters of our universe.

It's fair to assume that mathematics emerged out of the need to make sense of increasingly complex social relations in tribal affairs.

Symmetry, equivalence, abstraction, relationships, order, growth, and decay: these are the fundamental concepts of mathematics.

Pure mathematicians must think like children to see what adults cannot imagine.

Ramanujan was a famous mathematician who relied on a spiritual deity to discover mathematics. He showed, definitively, mathematics is so much more than logic and thinking. It is spiritual, it is divine, it is godly work.

A complex mathematics problem is like a 1,000,000-piece puzzle.

In the United States mathematics is taught far more slowly than in Asia.

Asians are good at rote mathematics because they are more hardworking, have a legacy of rice farming, and have a high tolerance for mental anguish.

To be good at mathematics you must have the ability to sit quietly for long hours.

Proving a difficult proof gives an intellectual high like having sex gives an emotional one. Though, to be fair, most would rather have the latter than the former. But to a select breed, intellectual discovery is the ultimate.

If you want to play the stock market, you better learn to play with numbers first.

If you want to become good at mathematics, begin with arithmetic and geometry, move on to set theory and logic, graduate to algebra and geometry, and close with calculus. From there you can go anywhere you like, but remember it only gets more opaque, esoteric, and mystical.

Applied math is a great way to play with mathematics without feeling like a hapless academic.

Great mathematicians are like great composers.

The best ideas in mathematics connect many different areas in one unifying theorem.

Most Americans should be taught arithmetic, statistics, and probability, instead of calculus, calculus, calculus.

Everyone loves mathematics when it comes to money.

The best mathematician to ever play the stock market is Jim Simons of Renaissance Technologies.

If you find yourself very bored by advanced mathematics you may be an idiot.

If you find yourself very smug by advanced mathematics you may be a nerd.

If you find yourself very blissed out by advanced mathematics you may be a genius.

Mathematics is a great tool for developing science, but a terrible substitute.

There are equations behind the great songs, behind the great paintings, and behind the great books, it's known as creativity, but behind creativity is the mathematics of creation.

Even artists use mathematics.

The mathematics of love is a multi-dimensional matrix of differential equations with constantly changing variables and infinite perturbations from the outside. In other words, it's complicated.

CHAPTER 12 – PHYSICS

The fundamental nature of the universe is best expressed in physics.

Without a deep understanding of physics, we would not have planes, trains, and automobiles.

Advances in physics are being withheld from the general population by the Military Industrial complex. There is a physics beyond want, beyond need, beyond imagination available to us and yet invisible to us.

The most interesting physics is the most taboo physics, namely the physics of teleportation, of time travel, of transmutation, of UFOs, of zero-point energy devices, of inter-dimensional portals.

Modern physics has gone looking for fantastical theories of the universe like a madman lost in the woods looking for sasquatches. But what all the greats knew, Oliver Heaviside, J.J. Thompson, Ernest Rutherford, and last but not least, Tesla, was simply this:

To understand the universe you must observe it, you must perceive it, you must play with it, you must poke it, you must not impose your mental biases on it, you must not impose your ideologies on it, and you must not condemn it to your fancy mathematical theories; in other words, you must Experiment, Experiment, Experiment. The truth will only come then. Let the physical reality dictate the mathematics and not the other way around.

What physics textbooks don't show is all the blood, sweat, and tears behind the elegant, direct, and profound theories, equations, and laws.

Bob Lazar is an example of a great experimental physicist. And like Galileo, a great example of a persecuted physicist. But a great rule of thumb emerges—study closely the persecuted physicists, their findings may be more exciting than the multitude of rent-seeking academics in ivory institutions.

The physics of war is the most impactful physics on Earth, though, it need not be.

There has been a great brain drain in physics, where the drain leads to Wall Street, and the brains make it rain...

If you stand on the shoulders of giants to see far, as Sir Isaac Newton declared, don't you risk falling and hurting yourself, after all giants are pretty tall???

Instead of a Manhattan Project to design more and more powerful weapons, why not a Manhattan Project to design more and more powerful energy distribution systems, the latter is the mark of progress and the former, the mark of madness...

Some of the great advances in Quantum Physics would not have been possible without the great Ancient Wisdom and Texts of India.

The physics approach to problem solving is wonderful in

all domains except for those that are governed by the heart.

The problem with modern physics is it's obsessed with breaking matter down into smaller and smaller pieces. The nature of this universe is such that the deeper you dig the greater the mess you make. The truth is, we will find more and more particles, possibly an infinite array, in our quest to find fundamental particles.

Where physics should focus more now, is not on the endless quest for fundamental particles, but on the useful quest of fundamental relationships, namely those between matter, across time and space, and with solutions for seemingly impossible tasks by addressing fundamental questions like: What is gravity? What is the relationship between electro-magnetism and time? Electromagnetism and gravity? What role does plasma play in new propulsion systems? How can we operationalize quantum entanglement? What is the nature of the akash, or the ether as some call it? What experiments can we do to test the possibility of time-travel, teleportation, and meta-material manipulation? These are the questions that I wonder about, and I wish more hardcore physicists and billionaires did too. Instead of cockamamie missions to Mars. No one wants to live on fucking Mars! It's all a big budgetary swindle and cultural misdirection. We live on Earth, it is the garden of Eden, why don't we worry about making it cleaner and healthier for our children by cleaning up our energy. And that's only going to happen when we clean up our physics.

People that poo-poo the bible as fantastical, mythological, ridiculous, unbelievable, absurd, unscientific, and childish have never studied Quantum Mechanics, Quantum Chromodynamics, and Particle Physics.

Great physics discoveries have been made by great physicists stealing concepts or ideas from fields far away from physics. Feynman once famously had an insight about quantum particle spins in a strip club. Everyone has always known such clubs could be fun for a man, but who knew they could also be so illuminating.

The key to understanding physics is a clear and keen perception married to a childlike curiosity.

The laws of thermodynamics are only laws which apply to certain earthly materials and circumstances. But like the laws of men, there are different rules in different places. Most have just not become aware of those faraway places filled with far away beings.

CHAPTER 13 – ENGINEERING

The one thing the engineers can't seem to figure out is this: how come the business guys make more money than the former while not being good at anything in particular, and certainly not good at solving technical problems. Exceptional engineers great at business, like Elon Musk, are not being addressed. Nerds are.

Engineering in its essence means setting things up they we want subject to the constraints of the world.

There is an intellectual hierarchy to engineers, at the bottom are the civil engineers, at the top are the electrical and nuclear, in the middle the mechanical and industrial, at the top today are the software gurus. But such hierarchies are always shifting in accordance with the dominant and emergent technologies of the day. The day will soon come when Quantum Engineers are the most prestigious, but not before biomechanical ones have their day in the sun.

Advanced engineering today is done by P. hd.'s, in the past it was done by master craftsmen.

Why doesn't this bridge collapse? That is a question of engineering. How can we make this bridge cross this chasm? That is a question of engineering. What is a bridge and how can we make one? That is a question of ingenuity.

Physics and Engineering are twin brothers with slightly different personalities.

The greatest engineers could visualize their machines before ever a single screw was twisted or single joint welded.

It remains to be seen whether human engineering can go truly beyond the wheel.

The only kind of engineering that does society no good is financial engineering.

The truly groundbreaking engineers never attain to popular acclaim. Have you ever heard of Rudolf Diesel? I imagine not. Have you ever heard of Henry Ford? I imagine so. I wonder why? First, man over the top usually gets lost to a hail of bullets and history. In war it's certainly true, perhaps, it's true in engineering too.

Tesla is the first publicly traded car company to make no internal combustion engine powered vehicles. It's the dawn of a new age. And that age is electrical.

If it weren't for engineers, we'd still be huddled together around fires in caves.

If it weren't for engineers, we'd still be killing each other with sticks and stones and all our bones.

If it weren't for engineers, we'd still be paddling canoes without shoes down blues.

If it weren't for engineers, we'd still be happy naked and fun but hungry and baked in the sun.

If it weren't for engineers, we'd still be talking not texting and sexting and wondering what ever happened to the time.

In some ways the most beautifully engineered machines in the world are mechanical watches from Switzerland.

Software engineering, as powerful as it is, is not as physically satisfying as mechanical engineering.

A great mechanism can change the world.

The best paying jobs in engineering fifty years from now will be for robot repair technicians, that's assuming the robots can't fix themselves, because in that case we're all screwed.

The ideal engineer is a renaissance man. The ideal engineer is a renaissance woman. The ideal engineer is a person without bias, with energy, and full of curiosity.

The human body is the most advanced machine ever engineered, I just wish I could take a look at the owner's manual, or better yet have a word with the inventor.

The more complexity a machine has the more fragile it is.

The less complexity a machine has the more robust it is.

Moving parts is a good proxy for complexity.

The heart and soul of a great engineering problem solver is a tinkerer. An endless tinkerer. A long days and late nights tinkerer. Success and failure become irrelevant when you're tinkering because there's no end in sight, no design too perfect, and no device ever finished.

An engineer is someone who is good at math and science but isn't a nerd. In other words, he's willing to have a pint in the night after a hard day's ways.

Just as there is pedigree in politics and power, art and athletics, music and mathematics, so too is there pedigree in engineering. Knowledge doesn't just pass from books to people, it also passes from people to people, from people to people, from people to people, across the generations and even down through nations.

CHAPTER 14 – LONELINESS, SOLITUDE, AND STILLNESS

For some, there is no greater pain than being alone for extended periods of time. Indeed, people can't stand solitude to such an extent that's it's the ultimate form of punishment short of death inside a prison.

Being alone can either lead to your enlightenment or your enslavement. The choice is yours.

In truth, we are always alone, even in the company of others, all the touching and so on is a temporary reprieve because physicality is inherently bounded, limited, and separated. Is there a way to be one with all beyond the physical?

Being alone is lovely if you can't stand other people. Being alone is terrible if you love other people. And being alone is neither if you don't think when you're alone, and instead just be.

If you want to get somewhere fast, go alone. If you want to take your time, go with company.

Lonely people tend to have a lot of hobbies and past times. Lonely people tend to read many books. Lonely people tend to be introverts. Loneliness can become solitary when one dissolves totally into their activities or better yet, their being.

Few professions pay you to be alone for long periods of time. I can think of one notable exception—Fiction Writers.

The work from home era augurs to be one of the loneliest eras of human enterprise, I hope for your sake it doesn't last long.

Most people dislike being alone so much they'd rather keep a job with people they like that pays less than have a job with people they don't like but pays more. Money-psychos are the exception.

Long haul truckers know a thing or two about loneliness.

Long periods of aloneness can either make or break you.

Long hikes alone in the wilderness put your existence into its proper perspective.

When you choose to be alone, that's peaceful. When you're forced to be alone, that's torture.

The ability to work alone for long periods of time has always been valuable, but in today's technotronic-computer-infotainment age it's practically a superpower. Who can compete with the computer programmer who can sit typing away furiously for 16 hours straight? Who can compete with the writer who can sit typing away furiously for 16 hours straight? Who can compete with the algorithmic trader who can sit typing away furiously for 16 hours straight? Who can compete with obsession, passion, and grit? Who can compete with the all-night sitters?

Librarians and lawyers are people comfortable with solitude.

Lonely people tend to have rich introspective intellectual lives.

Social media has made loneliness seem less prevalent, but it's actually more prevalent than ever, and perhaps more poignant than ever given the prevalence of party lifestyles projecting through our phones.

Being able to sit comfortably, absolutely, and peacefully still is the shortest path to enlightenment, and the least sought.

It's been famously quipped that all of man's problems stem from his inability to sit quietly in a room alone. Perhaps it's true, but all of his solutions spring from this inability too.

The great meditators of the east could remain seated in one posture for months. This is a level of stillness unimaginable to a western mind.

There are a few souls for whom solitary confinement brought enlightenment. But they are few and far between. For most it brought only madness.

Superman had his fortress of solitude, what place of solace

do you have?

There are consecrated spaces around this world for which stillness is possible even for the uninitiated.

A lone wolf keeps all that he kills, but shares none of the thrills.

In nature being alone meant risking death, in modern life it's the de facto state. Thus, the body can often switch into a flight or fight kind of stress response when you spend a lot of time alone, especially for city dwellers (rural environments tend to put even the lonely mind and body at ease). The antidote to this is go outside, go for a walk, volunteer, join a gym, join a sports club, join a book group, join anything with people and forget about your personal melodrama because in the end it won't even matter to you on your deathbed.

There's no question loneliness can be painful. There's no question pain can be joyless. There's only one question that matters though, will you turn it around?

CHAPTER 15 – PHILOSOPHY AND ISM-NESS

Western philosophy is famous for asking big questions and providing small answers.

Eastern philosophy is famous for asking small questions and providing big answers.

No philosophy is infamous for asking no questions and providing no answers.

A great man once said, "Modern Liberalism is a mental disorder." Addendum: Any -ism is a mental disorder waiting to happen.

The fictional movie character Ferriss Bueller once famously said, "I don't believe in isms, I believe in myself." Not a bad way to live if you want to go thru life with relative ease. But it's easier said than done.

If you identify with any kind of -ism, you should tread carefully, life will not be what it seems, and you may never achieve your dreams.

The big philosophy of 2020 is "woke" philosophy. The

great irony is that its proponents are woefully asleep.

Atheism, Theism, Communism, Capitalism, Feminism, Masculinism, Conservatism, Liberalism, Hedonism, Asceticism, Libertarianism, Marxism, Quietism, Loudism, Reductionism, Expansionism, Stoicism, Emotionalism, Ageism, Racism, Antisemitism, Classism, Cisgenderism, Colonialism, Ethnocentrism, Nativism, Jingoism, Sizeism…ism this and ism that, ism this and ism that, ism this and ism that. The more you label the farther we get from each other, the farther we get the more we label, you get so far, and no one can sit together at the bar.

There are many great philosophers today which can be found on twitter, but they seem so bitter.

If everyone lived by their own philosophy perhaps the world would be a better place.

There are many places where philosophy just must work. Exercise philosophy. Martial arts philosophy. Sports philosophy. You can't hide behind convoluted meanings and abstract logic in these endeavors. The beauty of the physical is that it tells no lies.

Plato is not the Spanish word for plate. And Socrates is not a brand of socks. But Nietzsche did go crazy.

Bite Sized Philosophy for the Maniacally Busy:

Plato's *Republic* can be summed up in a few short sentences:

A bunch of Greek drinking buddies get together to discuss justice and the ideal city. They argue, as Greeks are prone to do, endlessly. The famous Socrates makes his case that the soul is made of three parts: rational, spirited, and appetitive, each corresponding to thought, emotions, and bodily desire. From this premise, Socrates builds the ideal form of government. Long story short, the ideal form is a society ruled by philosopher-kings, doh! What a surprise, the philosopher wants to run the show. Nevertheless, you can't hate the guy, he does shit on every other form of government too, like democracy, which he says leads to tyranny because people desire freedom at the expense of others and are ruled by their appetites and not reason. And judging by the state of America in 2020, he may have been on to something.

Aristotle's *Ethics* can be summed up in a few short sentences:

The good life, the happy life, is a life of virtuous action. Virtuous action is not an absolute thing. But a good heuristic for taking virtuous action is the golden mean, in other words take the middle road, moderation and all that. Pretty simple, why did the guy need to write such a long-convoluted book? For posterity of course!

Nietzsche's *Beyond Good and Evil* can be summed up in a few short sentences:

Despite the title, not really much on good or evil. Mostly talking shit on philosophers, the "herd" of dumb people, and women. All in all, Nietzsche manages to offend the most people in the fewest words. Admirable for its audacity, if disagreeable for its paucity of positivity.

Machiavelli's *The Prince* can be summed up in a one line:

Game of Thrones—the user's manual.

Adam Smith's *The Wealth of Nations* can be summed up in a few economic quips:

Division of labor good. Productivity increases better. Invisible hand of the market best thing ever (and it feels so good!).

Karl Marx's *Das Kapital* can be summed up in a few revolutionary remarks:

Division of labor bad. Productivity increases demeaning. Invisible hand of the market feels like getting groped. Workers of the world unite!

God's *The Bible* can be summed up in a few short sentences:

God gives paradise. Humans screw it up. God punishes humans. God forgives humans by sending his only son to save them. His only son saves them. People take the message and run with it.

Marcus Aurelius's *Meditations* can be summed in a stoic saying:

Shit happens, expect it, and deal with it with a smile.

Rene Descartes's *Discourse on Method* can be summed in one line actually:

I fart therefore I am. Or in Latin for you brainy types: *Crepito, ergo sum.*

Lao Tzu's *Tao Te Ching* can be described simply:

Be chill and you'll have all the thrills and none of the frills.

Sun Tzu's *The Art of War* can be summed up violently as follows:

Crush your enemies by crook or by hook, keep them guessing, and remember the art of war is reception**deception**-inception.

CHAPTER 16 – STUPIDITY

A famous fictional character once said, "Stupid is as stupid does." I never quite understood that one. I guess I'm stupid.

Of all the human pain and suffering in the world, I reckon the lion's share of it comes from stupidity.

Ignorance is the disease which ails us most of all, not heart disease, not diabetes, not cancer, not alcoholism, not drug addiction, not depression, its ignorance of ourselves, ignorance of our true nature, ignorance of each other, ignorance of how to be, how to act, and how to live.

The more you admit how little you know, the farther you'll go.

Animals are stupid, but they don't have to go see therapists, like us smart humans.

The smarter you are, the more likely you are to identify with your intelligence. The dumber you are, the more likely you are to identify with your body. Typically, the former has mental breakdowns, and the latter has physical breakdowns. But the simpler folk definitely have more fun in the process!

They say an IQ below 85 means you're not qualified for

any modern job. Yet many organisms with a zero IQ can survive all fours seasons, feed themselves and their families, and never worry a day in their lives. So, why do us humans make such a big deal about it?

For most people, in life you start off stupid and you end up stupid.

It's fair to say stupid actions are those that have negative long-term consequences. But it's also fair to say stupid actions are those that have positive short-term consequences. Ohh, the conundrum!

Everyone can say unprotected sex is a stupid idea in hindsight, but in the sight of the moment it's probably the greatest thing since sliced bread.

Most skateboarders you'll come across are edgy idiots.

Most surfers you'll come across are enlightened idiots.

Most race car drivers you'll come across are ecstatic idiots.

Stupidity a poem:

Being a drug lord is really stupid idea if you don't like prison, killing people, or looking over your shoulder on a daily basis.

Being a doctor is a really stupid idea if you don't like blood, sick people, and hospitals.

Being a bodybuilder is a really stupid idea if you don't like steroids, dieting, and lifting weights.

Being a lawyer is a really stupid idea if you don't like

reading, writing, and extemporaneous speaking in suits.

Being an engineer is a really stupid idea if you don't like math, science, and tools.

Being a Navy Seal is a really stupid idea if you don't like swimming, kicking-ass, and guns.

Being the President of the United States is a really stupid idea if you don't like getting no sleep, being hated by half the country, and wielding the power to end the world.

Being a world-famous writer is a really stupid idea if you don't like writing, giving short poetic speeches before audiences, and travel.

Being a world-famous chef is a really stupid idea if you don't like shopping for food, cooking food, and chaotic kitchens.

Being a yoga instructor is a really stupid idea if you don't like teaching, stretching, and rubber mats.

Being a journalist is a really stupid idea if you don't like not making money, travel, and a lack of job security.

Being a software engineer is a really stupid idea if you don't like sitting for long hours, typing on a keyboard, thinking about discrete mathematical problems.

Being a pure mathematician is a really stupid idea if you don't like solving math problems, number 2 pencils, and logic.

Being a physicist is a really stupid idea if you don't like solving physics problems, vector calculus, and free-body diagrams.

Being a chemist is a really stupid idea if you don't like the periodic table of elements, rubber gloves, and Bunsen burners.

Being an entrepreneur is a really stupid idea if you don't like failure, rejection, and massive success after years of suffering.

Being a dentist is a really stupid idea if you don't like high pay, minimal hours because most of the work is done by your nurses, and everyone secretly hating your guts.

Being a traveler is a really stupid idea if you don't like planes, trains, and cars.

Being a stand-up comedian is a really stupid idea if you don't like telling jokes, people not laughing at your jokes, years of obscurity and poverty.

Being a bureaucrat is a really stupid idea if you don't like rules, protocols, and doing essentially nothing for 8 hours.

Being a construction worker is a really stupid idea if you don't like working in the sun, sweating in the sun, and working with large machines and large men in the sun.

Being a rancher is a really stupid idea if you don't like horses, cow manure, and wearing cowboy boots and hats.

Being anything you don't want to be is a really stupid idea if you don't plan to live forever, never die, or otherwise live as deified immortal.

In closing......I'm really stupid so take everything I say with a grain of salt and a pinch of cyanide.

CHAPTER 17 - HISTORY

If you aren't careful, you can be fooled into thinking history is leather-bound books, professors with patches on their suit jackets, and long lectures in old lecture halls.

It's a well stated truism that history is written by the victors. That's a bit of a euphemism. History is written by the killers, the best and the brightest, but killers all the same.

The only way to sort history out once and for all, one way or the other, is someone's got to invent a time machine and then immediately start a time travel tourism industry. Only hiccup might be that they don't have Airbnb in the past. Oh well, I guess we can just brand it as Adventure Tourism.

Most people get their history from television and movies. Which explains why the world is in such a sorry state of affairs at the moment. But then again if you know your history, you know it always seems to be in a sorry state of affairs.

His story, my story, your story, our story, so many damn stories, can someone at least pass me a pint!

A Student once asked his Professor, "Sir, what's the best way to study a given period of history?" To which the Professor replied, "The best way to study the history of a certain period is to read everything written in that period." The Student gave a look askance, as if to say, *you got to be kidding* me. The Professor merely shrugged his shoulders and said, "Hey, you asked, that's the best way to do it." Now the Student was determined to get a real answer, "What's the best way to do it within the time limits of this courses' term paper?"

Now the Professor lights up, "Well, that's easy, just cite this Professor's books on the subject and heap praise and you'll certainly guarantee at least a B"

If you want to read about the Roman Empire, certainly read Gibbons' *Decline and Fall of the Roman Empire*, but by god man, read the writers and thinkers of those times, Plutarch, Cicero, Aurelius, Virgil. Nothing beats the grounds eye view.

People tend to neglect history nowadays in the world of trading and finance, especially among the amateur class of traders, but it is the greatest teacher when it comes to the mania and madness of the markets. And in receiving those teachings, if nothing else, you may gain an advantage over other men in the making of money.

The history of a city can tell you everything you need to know about the place of its people in the present.

The cycles of history repeat like the cycles of nature, like clockwork for one like the weather for the other.

History is heresy when it stops serving the powers that be and it tries to set the people free.

The most relevant history to any person is the history of their family, unfortunately except for the royals and the elites, it's the history most sorely lacking in understanding.

The history they teach in middle school and high school textbooks is not a lot different from the excrement that comes out of large angus bulls after they eat.

Don't believe the governments account of the recent past, not because you want to be a contrarian or a conspiracy theorist, or whatever label they use now, but because history has shown, time and time again, governments lie to cover their own ass, in this respect they are just like you!

The wisdom of the sages is the wisdom of the ages, and the ages can be found in the pages... of history.

Reading the biographies of great men and women is the best form of self-help, for one you learn some history, for two you learn some hacks, for three you learn some heroes.

History is filled with great heroes and villains, but in truth, they are just people, the ideal perception is to neither look up to them nor look down on them, but by God please learn something from them.

Be skeptical of media praised history books that come out within the last 5 years.

Reading Wikipedia articles does not make you a history buff, but it does make you look like one.

Because everything ever written about history is only a click away, it's not more memorization we need, but more understanding.

Don't just read about the history of your people, your place, your philosophies, read those of others, often times, reading the history of others is more illuminating than reading our own history.

If you read enough history, you know there's nothing new under the sun. So, what I say is this, just go have fun. And maybe, you'll make your history worth remembering a ton.

CHAPTER 18 – LOSING

Ahh, now we come to it, everyone's favorite subject: losing. What a bruising, losing. We all go through it, yet none admit it. Ahh, now we come to it, everyone's favorite subject: losing. You feel you're cruising, then losing. What a pain, in every game. Ahh, now we come to it, everyone's favorite subject: losing. It feels like oozing, all that losing. We like to win, but it's all that sin, losing, losing, losing.

Losing in love feels like losing in the casino if you'd wagered your soul instead of your roll.

I've had many great teachers, wonderful professors, profound gurus, but none could teach or motivate better than losing.

When you lose in the markets you lose your shirt, when you lose in life you lose everything.

Some losses you can comeback from, others you can't, thankfully for most of us the majority of losses are in the former category and not the latter.

If you don't hate losing, you're not human.

If you don't use losing, you're not going to win.

If you like losing, good news for you, there's plenty more where that come from.

Being competitive just means you hate losing more than you like winning.

The feeling of losing is ten times worse than the feeling of winning is good.

It's a curious truism, some of the biggest losers in politics ended up becoming some of the biggest winners, namely Abraham Lincoln, who lost a handful of races before winning big. Although it's the cemetery of losers who never got back up again that should concern you because we don't write books or make movies about them.

If you like taking risks, then prepare to take losses, and more importantly be prepared to pick yourself back up again.

There are born losers, perhaps this particular life for them is about losing, in any case, try not to get in their way if you're competing against them.

Often times, all it takes to be a loser is ignorance of how to breathe properly, especially in tough situations.

We love sports because losing happens fast, and therefore winning could be right around the corner.

We hate office life because losing happens slow, and therefore winning could be down the hall, down the stairs, around the corner, and out the front door because your ass just got fired!!!

There are certain things where losing means your winning: bodyweight, inhibitions, and fears to name a few.

When you're in a losing groove, its best to stop moving and wait for another song.

If you're a man, the loss of a female partner is a sting that cuts deep into your amygdala. If you're a woman, the loss of a male partner is a sting that cuts deep into your amygdala. If you're a player (either sex) the loss of a partner is like free agency for LeBron James.

Childhood losses haunt us the longest, the hardest, and the deepest.

Bad Luck is a big part of losing, just like Good Luck is a big part of winning.

The habits of the loser are many, to name a few: laziness, poor diet, willful ignorance, paralyzing subconscious fears and doubts, lack of focus, lack of perseverance, lack of perception, drug and alcohol abuse, association with other losers, over-consumption of mass media, and most important of all—a lack of curiosity. No one habit can derail you but start stacking these habits together like a bunch of pancakes and you'll be well on your way.

If you're a born loser, then your best bet is to burn off all your karma. Easier said than done, but that's my two cents.

Arrogance and losing are like father and son.

Perhaps the most painful thing about losing is knowing someone else won. Envy is a son-of-a-bitch. You're better off being enlightened and then it's all fun and games and you won't feel the need to call people names, cause that's just lames.

CHAPTER 19 – WINNING

Winners work, losers worry.

Whether you love him or hate him, it's hard to argue that Donald Trump isn't a born winner.

Winning is the worst teacher but the best companion.

Winning a beautiful woman's heart feels like winning the lottery for a romantic, it feels like winning a war for a warrior, and it feels like making money for a businessman, in short it feels great.

Whether you win or lose doesn't matter, said losers the world over.

The instinct to win, is the instinct to survive, the instinct to kill, to ensure one's preservation and procreation. It's the instinct of nature, by nature, for nature.

Working out is a small win, which if done regularly can create a lifetime of winning, in whatever your chosen field.

Early age success in sports can propel one to success in other fields and often does, unless you are a simpleton content with early glories, nothing wrong or right about it either way.

An addiction to winning will never go out of style, never be socially repressed, and never not be rewarded no matter the system.

To win a war is the ultimate victory in the affairs of men and people.

To win mastery of the self is the ultimate victory in the affairs of men and women.

To win enlightenment goes beyond winning and losing, beyond life and death, beyond everything.

People that win the lottery end up losing in other ways.

To win consistently and persistently takes perspiration by the bucketful, which takes a great sense of humility because winning is the strongest psychedelic drug on earth, and it can have hallucinatory effects that would make Timothy Leary blush.

Winning in the financial markets is a great vindicator of intelligence or luck or both.

The biggest win you can have in life is in the relationships between your family and your friends.

There are a lot of sore losers but far fewer sore winners.

Many professions and career fields are subject to what Nassim Taleb calls, "superstar effects", in other words LeBron

James, Tiger Woods, and Roger Federer take all the gold while you get old. Thankfully, most professional paths only have mild superstar effects. Why do you think the risk averse gravitate toward them so strongly? Fear of extinction is a son-of-a-gun.

Winning a Poem:

Winning an endurance race is a testament to a person's tolerance for pain.

Winning a rat race is a testament to a person's tolerance for bullshit.

Winning a car race is a testament to a person's ability to focus with the Grim Reaper sitting in the passenger seat.

Winning an Olympic swimming race is a testament to a person's tolerance for monotony.

Winning the college admissions race is a testament to a person's capacity for hyperbole and planning.

Winning the startup race is a testament to a person's intelligence, networking skills, and upper-middle class upbringing.

Winning the arms race is a testament to a country's military, industry, and banking system.

Winning a political race is a testament to a person's lack of ethics, cunning, and speechifying charisma.

Winning the publishing race is a testament to a person's marketing, connections, and luck.

Winning the big tech interview race is a testament to a person's problem solving skills, left-wing virtue signaling, and resume.

Winning a professional golf tournament is a testament to a person's skill, caddy, and luck.

Winning the restaurant race is a testament to a person's

cooking skill, location, and location.

Winning the movie race is a testament to a person's screenplay, actors, and studio marketing campaign.

Winning anything really is a testament to hard work, luck, and luck.

If there was a cheat code so you could win at everything, every time in Life, would you have turned it on a long time ago???

A life spent winning is a life spent losing out on all kinds of valuable lessons. But that's just loser speak because who wants to learn lessons when you could be winning?

CHAPTER 20 - CONSPIRACY THEORIES, MEMES, AND INTERNET CULTURE

So many theories, or are they just queries, all these theories, conspiracy theories. Over a beer ok, but not in the office. Over a doobie, definitely, but not in the middle of the game. Over a meal, what kind of deal? Please, save the conspiracy theories for your weird 4chan friends.

Some people would have you believe conspiracies are theories, but they are mistaken, conspiracies are thoughts, held by more than one person over more than one time period and one place.

Conspiracies are the modus operandi of the world, that's why the Mainstream Media ridicules them so much.

Statistically speaking most conspiracy theories are B.S., but you could say that about a lot of things.

Seeing conspiracies in everything is just as foolish as seeing no conspiracies in anything.

The internet imageboard Politically Incorrect on 4chan is oftentimes the worst thing about the internet, and every now and again the best thing for freedom of information.

The 2016 Presidential Election was the first quadrennial contest decided by internet memes.

Internet culture is virtually synonymous with youth culture because youths have more time and curiosity about the world.

A good conspiracy will take up a moment of your time. A great one will take up a night. A legendary one will make you rich.

The most famous, least questioned, and best understood of all conspiracies is the drug cartel.

Marriage is a conspiracy, a good one if it lasts, and a bad one if it goes by too fast.

The most important conspiracy in the world is the energy conspiracy. The least important conspiracy in the world is the one you make in your mind. The funniest conspiracy in the world are the ones that defy logic, like lizards that run the world.

Finance is a conspiracy to take money from working people and give it to thinking people so they can make rich people richer.

The government is a conspiracy to tax people and take their freedoms in exchange for security and stability.

Professional sport is a conspiracy to take peoples time

and money in exchange for entertainment, mostly in the form of vicarious living, hopes and dreams, and speculative wagers.

Not a totally original thought, but all professions are a conspiracy against the common man.

The corporation is a conspiracy to monopolize money, power, and influence in a certain industry of a certain industry group of a certain sector of a certain economy.

The military is a conspiracy to kill on a mass scale with standardized methods of command and control.

The publishing industry is a conspiracy to exchange information, sometimes propaganda, sometimes wisdom, for money and time.

Netflix is a conspiracy to get young people laid and others paid.

Fast food is a conspiracy to satisfy hunger at the expense of health.

A movie theater is a conspiracy to upcharge people on dates for candy, popcorn, and soft drinks to pay down commercial real estate debt to a bank.

A bank is a conspiracy to make money out of money, some people call this interest, what they ought to call it is magic.

A newspaper is a conspiracy to spin events and history in favor of its owners for the entertainment of its readers.

Congress is a conspiracy to siphon money from the government for the benefit of its inhabitants at the expense of its constituents.

The Supreme Court is a 9-person conspiracy to let legal scholars decide the fate of millions under the guise of caselaw.

The Presidency is a conspiracy to let one man decide the fate of the world for 4 years under the advisement of bureaucrats, billionaires, and bankers.

Life is a conspiracy to suffer, succeed, and survive in a perpetual cycle unless…

Royalty is a conspiracy to intoxicate the masses with intoxicated people.

A health fad is a conspiracy to convince people they can eat like shit and not look like shit.

College is a conspiracy to educate poorly and party entirely.

Social Media is a conspiracy to promote stupidity in the name of socializing.

Literature is a conspiracy to pay a person who plays with words because most people can't play with them themselves.

4chan is a conspiracy to poison the mind under the guise of forbidden information.

The diamond ring industry is a conspiracy to sell you worthless rocks in the name of invaluable love.

The pharmaceutical company is a conspiracy to sell you poison because age old remedies work too slow and you don't even know how they grow.

Any man-made institutional, educational, industrial system is a conspiracy to enslave not enlighten people, exceptions exist but most don't persist.

CHAPTER 21 – WOMEN

The fall of a man always starts with a woman. The rise of a man always starts with a woman. The life of a man is for a woman.

A good woman is there to pick up a man after he falls.

Women are natural caretakers, of pets, of children, of people, of organizations, of places, of societies.

The rise and fall of a civilization can be charted with the rise and fall of its' women.

Most women are not interested in STEM fields nor are they any good at them compared to men.

Women that are stand-up comedians tend to be either tough lesbians or Jewish women impersonating a man.

A beautiful woman can start a war and an ugly one can end one.

Women can withstand more pain than men, but their bodies break down faster under stress.

A good mother is a blessing to the world. A bad mother is

a curse to the world. And a great mother is a portal to the divine.

Women are just as smart as men, just in different ways.

Serious feminist women have issues related to male authority figures that originate in childhood (gee what a surprise).

The surge in tattoos among women is a sorry sight for conservatives and a promising portent for progressives.

Women are wonderful listeners and litigators because they love language; after all, it was their only weapon for millennia.

Women are obsessed with social media because it preys off their natural inclination toward relationship, vanity, and gossip.

The wisdom of women is the wisdom of the world.

Working women have an uphill battle to be recognized and respected.

Womanhood is under assault just as bad as manhood is, and surprisingly much of the attack from certain high classes of women.

The dutiful wife has been demonized to the point of being considered a relic of the past by some.

The luscious paramour has been glamorized to the point of being considered the way of the future by some.

The intelligent and honor-bound woman has been written off by some but will rule the day forever.

Getting married to the right woman is better than winning the lottery. Getting married to the wrong woman is worse than losing a fortune in the stock market. Never getting married to a woman is like never playing the lotto or the stock market, not a lot of fun and a little too boring for some.

A woman who can cook well never has to worry if her husband won't come home.

A cruel woman's words can destroy even the greatest men.

Chivalry died when chastity died.

A chaste woman is more valuable than 100 tons of gold and rarer too.

Female bartenders make the loneliness of drinking alone at a bar palatable because there is the potential for something more, and that potential makes the world go round.

If it weren't for women in this world, the sweetness would be gone.

If it weren't for women in this world, wars would go on forever.

If it weren't for women in this world, drunkenness would reign supreme.

If it weren't for women in this world, jokes would be far and few between.

If it weren't for women in this world, men would not dare so greatly.

If it weren't for women in this world, charities would go unfunded.

If it weren't for women in this world, all the forests would be lumbered.

If it weren't for women in this world, children would be miserable.

If it weren't for women in this world, there would be no world.

CHAPTER 22 – MEN

There are many common sayings which call man a beast. "Men are pigs." "Men are dogs." "Men are monkeys." And so on. But aren't men so much more? Can't they be divine? Why not say: "Men are gods." "Men are wise." "Men are gurus."

To be a man is to have a 6-inch brain.

To be a man is to fight for your right.

To be a man is to suffer nobly.

To be a man is to succeed ignobly.

To be a man is to fail.

To be a man is to win.

To be a man is to act.

To be a man is to wait.

To be a man is hunt.

To be a man is to nurture.

To be a man is to love a woman.

To be a man is to be betrayed by a woman.

To be a man is to be many things and yet hold it all together.

The strength of man lies in his heart, his head, and his heroism.

The weakness of man lies in his pride, greed, and lustfulness.

The greatness of man lies in his divine nature.

The demise of the west will come because men refuse to be strong anymore.

A great man can be a benefit to a million people. A small man cannot even be a benefit to himself. And the average man is somewhere in between.

What is manliness? At its core, it is moving forward with the Grim Reaper beside you, around you, and within you.

Why do men seek to conquer the world? So, many aims. Fame. Wealth. Women. But aren't they all the same? The transmutation of pain. Pleasure is the game.

Men can do many things better than women. Drinking for one. Working in the sun for some. And acting dumb in sum.

Men are great technical problem solvers because they've been practicing for millennia.

Civilization may be perpetuated through women, but there's no doubt it's built on the backs of men.

The vast majority of men do not pass on their genetics. And only a small minority pass them on prosperously.

The cultural war on men is an ongoing process because society is shifting to an autonomous artificial assembly.

Men do so much work for small pleasures.

Women can do virtually anything a man can do, but the difference is a man can do it better. Whereas there are many things a man cannot do that a woman can, giving birth to a child for one.

A cohort of loud drunk men always thinks it is having the best time compared to others.

Some women like misogyny, that's why men do it.

A good man is a good father, and a good father makes a good family, and a good family makes a great country.

Men are judged by their actions, remembered by their words, and mythologized through their lies.

The defining characteristic of great men is great luck.

More men today are lost than ever before. Some much so they don't even know it. You can tell by their stare into the glow.

The only reason men go on social media is to get laid.

The only reason men workout is to get laid.

The only reason men compete in sporting contests is to get laid.

The only reason men learn to use technology is to get laid.

The only reason men write books is to get laid.

The only reason men construct great works is to get laid.

The only reason men do anything of any significance is to

get laid, unless of course it's for other reasons, than by all means, keep lying to yourself.

CHAPTER 23 – ANIMALS

A child can learn a great deal about the world by watching animals in the wild.

Animals have all of the fun without any of the guilt.

Animals are dumb, instinctual, and simple creatures but they have a great deal of perception when it comes to certain things.

Snakes are the most perceptive animals on the planet. They also get a bad wrap because of the whole Adam and Eve fiasco.

When the lion kills, everyone gets fed.

A gorilla and his harem are not all that different from a playboy and his playmates.

Dogs may be man's best friend, but it begs the question who is his worst enemy? It must be the monkey mind and the lizard brain.

Creatures of the desert can teach you of subsistence.

Creatures of the ocean can teach you of persistence. Creatures of the mountains can teach you of overcoming resistance. And every creature can teach you of existence.

We are all ants with pants.

Every animal on this planet is better specialized than human beings will ever be, but it's their inability to generalize that keeps them from eating us alive.

One of my favorite conspiracy theories is that humans were genetically engineered by extraterrestrial engineers. The basic premise is aliens came down from the stars and turned a bunch of primates, chimpanzees and so on, into modern humans, with some iterations of course: Neanderthals, Cro-Magnons, and probably others lost to history. There's a spooky set of coincidences which supports this thesis. For one, the Bible talks of the Nephilim, which were the purported sons of angels/gods which fell from heaven and procreated with earthly women. But the Bible also says these creatures were all wiped out in the flood. Secondly, there's all the mass media which has represented this possibility. Most recently, the film Prometheus, where space explorers go looking for the Engineers of Humanity and (spoiler alert) find them. There are countless books, most notably those put out by Zecharia Sitchin, which describe a race of aliens known as the Anunnaki, who engineered humans specifically to mine gold. Interesting, especially considering our obsession with the precious metal since time immemorial. But his analysis could be construed to suffer from lookback-bias, in other words fitting the present to the past conveniently. And on and on it goes. I remain open-minded to the possibility, and doubtful of the preached science of evolution, especially where humans are concerned, we're just so damn different than every other animal on this planet.

Horse breeding is a great education in nature vs. nurture. And a slap in the face to those that think pedigree is petty. After all Kentucky Derby winners are bred before they're led.

The emergence of emotional support animals is welcome sign for the treatment of animals and a disconcerting one for the tenacity of humans.

Humans love to have dogs around because, unlike themselves, dogs are always in the Now.

When you look a horse in the eye you get a feeling there's someone looking back at you. I don't think you can say that about other animals, even dogs.

Dog spelled backwards is god.

Animal instinct is often more valuable than human genius.

There are animals that will eat you and animals that will love you, some people don't know the difference, usually carnies.

Don't feel sorry about killing animals if you have to, they live that way every day.

If you want to know what killer instinct is all about, watch tigers in the wild.

If you want to know what flexibility is all about, watch cats of all kinds.

If you want to know the strength of a vegetarian diet,

watch gorillas in the wild.

Living around wild animals bring a certain sense of peace, reality, and humility to ones' life.

If you find yourself in the presence of a momma griz, as in grizzly bear, if you can—play dead, if your quick—run, and if you must—fight to the death.

CHAPTER 24 – SMARTPHONES

A smartphone is a great way to kill time, and a terrible way to spend your life.

The attention span of the Millennial and Zoomer generation has gone down immensely because of the smartphone. Recall that previous generations, could focus on one task for 12 hours. Can you? By the way, I was looking at my Instagram feed while I wrote this. Sorry, just couldn't help myself.

I hate goddamned smartphones. And I hate people who use them constantly. And I hate the stupid shit people do on them while they are driving.

I love blessed smartphones. And I love the easy sex I can get when I use them. And I love the ego boost I get from people's likes of pictures I post from my mundane life.

The smartphones of today are a zillion times more useful than the mainframe computers of yesteryear. But the people that played with the latter sure are a helluva lot smarter than the people that play with the former.

Smartphones have been a boon for advertisers and a pain in the ass for drug lords.

In the not too distant future, smartphones will be redundant, just like telegraphs. Why you ask? Because people will have the option to get implants. Elon Musk just announced them. You didn't hear? Have you been living under a rock?

Most people will never realize their full potential because of their smartphones.

Due to smartphones, everyone can be a pedantic poindexter now, not just the brainiacs, nerds, and geeks of yore.

People are so addicted to their smartphones they'd gladly risk their lives while flying down a highway at 75 miles per hour in order to catch the latest episode of their favorite YouTube channel.

If you can go a day without your smartphone, you're basically as disciplined as a Navy Seal, by today's standards.

Few things can pull me off my smartphone, sex and drugs are two of them, the third I leave to your imagination.

Smartphones are sooo prevalent; I've even seen hobos with them.

Some women can make a living off a smartphone, a few a killing, and almost none can live without one.

Smartphones are the status-symbols of the 21st century.

You know Apple lost its way when it started adding more cameras to its phones. Since when is that innovation? Boy does the world miss Steve Jobs.

Samsung's smartphone strategy is simple: wait for Apple to release a new phone, and then make a copy of it with a bigger screen, better cameras, and more battery life. Voila!!!

Smartphones can make your life better if you're disciplined. But they can also make your life hell if you're dysfunctional.

Social media applications have changed tremendously since the advent of the smartphone. In some ways for the better, they're now more focused on documenting everyday life, instead of just endless online diversion. The catch-22 is people now spend as much of their time documenting life as living it. What this portends for the future of human interaction is anyone's best guess.

No greater cure for boredom has ever been invented than the smartphone.

No greater excuse for distraction has ever been invented than the smartphone.

No greater device has ever been invented than the smartphone.

On your smartphone is virtually all that's ever been written, recorded, or manifested by man. You could spend a million lifetimes going thru it all. And yet at the end of the day, all you would have done was collect a lot information. Such an existence would be a failure, even though it might bring untold riches and power. But then why do so many people carry-on with their heads craned forward like a bird picking at pellets as they meander thru life transfixed by a pale-blue screen?

With a smartphone you can order anything on God's green earth: food, books, office supplies, computers, other smartphones, routers, motorcycles, dogs, cats, monkeys, parrots, all kinds of exotic pets, plants, pots, pans, knives, swords, t-shirts, polos, dress shirts, jeans, jeans that stretch, jeans with holes in them, jeans with lots of holes in them, hats: baseball ones, cowboy ones, goofy ones, sandals, shoes, Nikes, Jordans, Converse, Adidas, Lucchese boots, Birkenstocks, companionship, massages with happy endings, sex, drugs, beer, kegs of beer, imported beer, craft beer, organic food, inorganic food, ingredients to make magic mushrooms, ingredients to make bombs, concert tickets, sports tickets, festival tickets, camping tickets, new cars, used cars, furniture, a new home, a new roommate, golf clubs, golf tee times, movie tickets, video games, video game consoles, vacations, hotel reservations, boats, trailers, recreational vehicles, historic tours, a new wife, a new gun, a sauna, gym equipment, televisions, medicine, psychological counseling, spiritual counseling, and on and on and on ad infinitum...BUT...BUT...BUT...you still can't order happiness, or joy, or bliss, or transcendence, or enlightenment because those aren't on Amazon's catalog yet...they're not in any catalog... they are only available to a certain kind of consciousness...and your consciousness is entirely your own making...from within.

CHAPTER 25 – FOOD

The fried and true is often tastier than the tried and true.

The key to cooking good salmon is low heat, a little butter, a little garlic, and a healthy serving of vegetables on the side. Season as necessary and particular to your palette.

Eating a diet rich in bread will to lesser or greater degrees depending on your lineage inflame your body.

The easiest way to lose weight without having to think about it, count calories constantly, or read a dozen glossy books or magazines is this: eat 70% fruits and vegetables and 30% lean meats, fish, and chicken, while drinking pure water. That's it. All the mania about diets and related fads is people avoiding the truth, avoiding reality, and avoiding the dark side of their eating habits.

The best food for cheat days is pizza, beer, wings, donuts, burgers, French fries, fried chicken, in other words, the standard American diet.

Mexican food is taking over America. The future of American dining is not McDonalds. It's a taco stand. And my taco stand is Taco Palenque.

Frying food destroys whatever health and vibrance is

present beforehand. Haven't you ever noticed how crummy you feel after eating fried food?

Eat vegetables as fresh as possible, ideally from your own garden and of your own hands. Next best, is fresh from the farmers market. Next best, is fresh from the grocery store.

If you are on the spiritual path, it is a tradition to keep the food intake down. Something like 24 mouthfuls of food with extensive chewing. Haven't you ever noticed how your energy is consumed by the process of digestion?

A super smoothie for muscle recovery is made of plenty of bananas, some whole milk, whey protein, and blueberries. Keep the size down per drink but the quantity high throughout the day. This will make it easier for your digestive system to assimilate the food and keep you energized throughout the day.

Calorie counting is fine, macro management is good, but nutrient nourishment is best.

Once every month, but ideally once every week, you should not touch a piece of food. Drink only water. Give your guts a rest. And focus on the questions that are really weighing on you as of late. A great deal of clarity comes with fasting. Ask yourself these types of questions while on the fast: am I doing what I want to be doing with my life? Are the people in my life energizing or are they energy vampires? Are habits conducive to my goals? Is my career where I want it to be? Is it time to start a business? Is it time to get a new job? What fears are holding me back? Really let it rip, don't hold back on this day.

If you want deeper clarity to sort out longer-standing life confusions, fast for a week with water and light snacking, fruit, and vegetables. Meditate every day, ideally in the morning and evenings. If you want to go deeper within, meditate three times a day for an hour at least.

Fasting for more than a week with only water I would only recommend to the most intense people with an absolutely burning desire to go beyond their physical limitations, psychological prisons, and get a taste of Enlightenment.

Breakfast should be whatever the hell you like. Eggs and bacon are all well and good. But don't you want life to be a little more interesting. Try eating pizza in the morning. Eat a big steak. Eat a hamburger. Eat a big hearty salad filled with salmon. Hell, have some barbeque with potato salad and beans. Break your nightly fast with a flash and see how free life can really be when you live like a marquis!

Life without good food is like sex without physical contact.

Anthony Bourdain elevated travel and food to a high art. He will be sorely missed by many, including myself. His replacements like the pompous, stoned, and inebriated grease ball Action Bronson are shadows of the lanky legendary laconic Bourdain. If you want a great read which on the surface is about food and the food business, read Kitchen Confidential, but you should really read it because a man bears his soul across its' pages.

The ultimate hangover cure is a cold beer in the morning with a hot stew, Mexican style menudo is optimal, but every people have their version.

The best way to put on mass as a hard gainer is a gallon of milk a day. If you can drink a gallon of milk a day, rest assured your skinny ass will gain weight. The only question is, will that weight be made of mostly muscle or fat?

Millennials and Zoomers don't want to eat shit food that Baby Boomers grew up on. There will come a time when McDonalds, Burger King, and Taco Bell will be replaced with places like Shake Shack, Sweet Greens, and Chipotle. The process has already begun.

Fast food will never die, it will just mutate, morph, and re-label itself, Organic, Ketogenic, Gluten-Free, Grass Fed, COVID tested, and on and on and on. But the best food will always be homemade. Do you know why? Because of a cliché of course. Food made with love has a special quality, dare I say, a mystical quality about it, and you know it and I know it even though we can't put our finger on it.

Eating breakfast for dinner is fun when you're young. Eating fast food whenever is too. But if you do both too long and too strong, your youth will be short lived, and your life will be short shift.

CHAPTER 26 - DRINKING, GETTING DRUNK, AND ALCOHOL

Getting drunk alone is great for a writer. Getting drunk alone is great for an artist. Getting drunk all the time is not great for anyone.

Nothing pairs better with meat over an open fire than a night of heavy drinking.

Drinking feels awfully good when you're tired of thinking.

The craft beer phenomena is a welcome sign of a new age, an age removed from one size fits all offerings. Bud Light and Miller Lite are certainly not going anywhere, and have their place, but drinking piss water is only great if you're on a diet or don't like beer.

Golf and drinking go together like restaurants and eating.

Money and drinking go together like oil and water.

Relaxing and drinking go together like working and

money.

Thinking and drinking go together like cats and dogs.

Sex and drinking go together like dancing and music.

Abuse and drinking go together like chips and salsa.

Heavy machinery and drinking go together like terrorists and airplanes.

Beaches and drinking go together like sailors and cussing.

Good times and drinking go together like money and luck.

For every dysfunctional alcoholic, there are 100 functional ones, and therein lies the rub.

Whether you go to the bar or the church or the gym or wherever, you're looking for happiness, you're looking for life to be something more, you're looking for a feeling of lightness, but the bar is so popular because it happens fastest there.

Jesus once said the "kingdom of heaven is within," for some people the kingdom of heaven is within a bottle of Jack.

The perfect combination of vices is a Crown and Coke.

Watching sports and drinking keeps large hordes of men from outright revolution day in and day out. The Romans called it Bread and Circuses, we Americans call it Hooters and Football.

Blue-collar men, white-collar men, blue-collar women, white-collar women, they all drink after work, what does that say about work?

The brilliance of the Catholic religion is that drinking is

incorporated into its rites from the start.

Many people would go mad without their sour mash.

Technically speaking, alcohol is poison. Which begs the question, why does poisoning yourself feel so good in the short-term and so bad in the long-term?

Without liquid courage the world population might be half of what it is today.

Las Vegas has many people to thank for its success, but there is one thing that deserves the lion's share of the credit: booze.

Russians love their vodka. Mexicans love their tequila. Japanese love their sake. Germans love their beer. Englishmen love their whisky. Hipsters love their IPAs. Frenchmen love their wine. And Brewers love all of the above.

The best bourbon in the world is Blanton's, accept no substitutes.

The best scotch in the world is Johnnie Walker Blue, accept no substitutes.

The tastiest tequila in the world is Patron, accept no substitutes.

If there was a cure for hangovers, the world would be drunk all the time.

Some people drink to forget. Some people drink to remember. Some people drink to dance. Some people drink to sit. Some people drink to write. Some people drink to think. Some people drink to talk. Some people drink to make love. Some people drink to get mad. Some people drink to get glad. In the end, what would life be if we couldn't drink, drink, drink?

Women today have never been more sauced on wine than ever before.

The beer belly of the North American male is the mark of middle-agedness, no-fucks-giveness, and easy living.

There once was a sage who refused all intoxicants. His austerity attracted him many ascetics. They went from town to town. They went from mountain to mountain. They traveled all around their country in the Far East. His followers loved him because he refused all earthly delights. And so, like this they went. Starving. Meditating. Starving. Meditating. Starving Meditating. Until, finally, the great sage, grew weary of walking, his skin hanging loosely, set himself down by a tree. Here he sat unmoving. He resolved to die or be enlightened. The latter did come shortly. Awakened at last. He began to eat again. Teaching too. Some followers left. Others stayed. One day they came upon a town. The great sage was invited into the tavern. He drank and drank and drank. The disciples were excited. We can drink too now! But arriving at the next town, the great sage walked over to the blacksmith. He drank a goblet full of molten steel. And looked upon his apostles and laughed and smiled. They shrank in awe and wonder. Some people can hold their drink better than others!

CHAPTER 27 - WEED, LSD, MUSHROOMS, AND PSYCHEDELIC ADVENTURES

Some people think there's nothing more refreshing than a beer after a long hard day's work. They may be right. But nothing beats a marijuana blunt on a cool night in nature.

If alcohol is jolly juice, then weed is creativity cider.

A time is fast approaching when the biggest Super Bowl commercials will be for cannabis products.

The problem with consistent cannabis consumption is the manifestation of a marginal memory.

The benefit with consistent cannabis consumption is the removal of reality as a restriction.

Smoking marijuana makes the mind hazy. It's appealing to a mind which is running 100 miles an hour all the time. You see, it's like driving in the fog, you have to slow down. Whereas normally, your mind is barreling down the highway at some obscene speeds. But the cost of going slow is arriving at your destination later than expected. That's the cost of losing clarity.

Marijuana may energize you, but on average, it lowers the level of activity a person engages in.

A lot of people are covering emotional and psychological trauma by smoking marijuana.

Good weed has the ability to bring someone back down to earth.

Taking LSD is like raising the volume on the amp of Life.

For better or worse, bad LSD trips are more conducive for changing or even transforming one's life for the better. The good LSD trips are just visual and energetic trips to pleasure island.

On LSD you notice things that were always there, but in a higher resolution.

If you take a large enough dose of LSD, the fabric of reality will be pulled back, and you'll either like what you see or want to flee.

When you take LSD, rest assured you are in good company, Steve Jobs of Apple fame, Watson and Crick of DNA discovery fame, and Aldous Huxley of writing fame, all took LSD in their lives, some more than others. And credit the substance to enlarging their view of life, the cosmos, and reality.

When you take LSD, rest assured you are in bad company too, Ted Kaczynski of Unabomber fame, Charles Manson of Hollywood murder rampage fame, and countless others you've never heard of and never will hear from all took LSD in their lives, some under coercion. And credit the substance to diminishing the fine line between sanity and insanity.

What's the moral of the story? LSD is not for you if you can barely handle yourself on a daily basis. LSD is for you if you can. And it's ok to have a bad trip, those often turn into positive trips when you let go of control and just ride the wave. There are more long-lasting modes of deep perception, but unfortunately to the western mind, they take too long. LSD is a fast pass to heightened perception. But it's like Airbnb, you may be able to fool yourself and others that you're living the high life by posting pictures on Instagram of your stay at a mansion by the lake, but deep down you know it won't last because you haven't done the work to deserve such a place.

On LSD, religion seems far less far-fetched, and your ignorance seems far, far, far stretched.

Mushrooms are more fun than LSD because nature worked out all the kinks outside of a lab.

Mushrooms brewed in honey tea are a smooth way to get some magic in your life.

Good vibes and bad vibes take on a deep new meaning when you're on magic mushrooms.

The beauty of magic mushrooms is they force you into a new mode of perception and intelligence. Why is this beautiful? It is beautiful because you have gone thru life up to a certain point thinking, feeling, and acting one way, but now you see there is another way to be. This is beautiful because it awakens you to the possibility of crafting yourself and your destiny thru your own hands.

On psilocybin mushrooms you may see things which will shock you, rock you, or otherwise unblock you from the sleep you've been in for so long.

The biggest mistake with mushrooms is taking it around the wrong people in the wrong place.

The best place to take mushrooms is in nature, in a safe environment with good people.

There's a reason alcohol is available on every street corner and mushrooms aren't. There's a reason cigarettes are available on every street corner and mushrooms aren't. There's a reason pills are available on every street corner and mushrooms aren't. The formers make good customers and the latter makes good creators. The formers make good sheep and the latter makes good shepherds. The formers diminish consciousness and the latter expands consciousness. So, make your choice.

CHAPTER 28 - MISCELLANEOUS MAXIMS

Never ask a car salesman if you need a new car.

The faster you can learn, the farther you can go, and the further you can grow.

The world is littered with starving artists, fat oligarchs, hungry dogs, and far too few badasses.

If you can't run, walk.
If you can't walk, crawl.
If you can't crawl, watch.

The art of inspired creation is being alone and happy.

The powers that be charge a fee for you to bee, so don't let them see and you'll live free.

If you can't keep yourself moving in the same direction for long you won't get anywhere of any consequence.

If you can't decide, sometimes flipping a coin is a great solution.

If you are struggling to overcome psychological challenges, then beginning with physical challenges is a good start and a great teacher.

If you've lost the motivation to take action in your life, then indulge yourself and sit in a room for an entire day in meditation. Don't do anything. Really show yourself what no action is like. If you find peace in it, then perhaps you should move to an ashram or a certain kind of temple. But if you don't find peace in it. If instead the anxiety of action still pulls you in. Then you know that the lack of motivation is just your own mind, your own making, and your own laziness. And therefore, you can become the master of your own motivation.

If you find yourself unable to sleep at night, then think.
If you find yourself unable to think,
then walk.
If you find yourself unwilling to walk,
Then do something boring, sleep will
Find you no matter how remote you are.

Wait not.
Waste not.
Work now.

A good liar will look you in the eye.
A great liar will smile while he does it.

The future, your future, changes moment to moment, with every decision in the present.

You don't have forever; you just have for now. Use it wisely!

Realization is when reality and thought have a baby in your mind.

You have to give love to get it. But you can only give it if you are it.

Life is fun once you realize how short it is.

If you expect the impossible, nothing is possible. If you only do what is possible, you'll never do the impossible. Life is a paradox like that.

Success is setting a goal and accomplishing it.

Perfectionism is your Ego telling you you're God.

Pragmatism is your soul realizing you're not.

Greatness is living by the latter.

Happiness is doing without expectations.

Winning is a symptom of working.

Losing is a symptom of laziness.

A comedy makes you laugh.

A tragedy makes you cry.

An epic makes you wonder why?

The eyes may be the windows into the soul. But feet tell

you how a person feels.

Shoes tell you where a person shops.

If you can close a deal before lunch, then you can play golf before dinner.

Misery is waiting for tomorrow when you could be living today.

When you are down look up.

When you are up don't stop.

When you are stuck dig deep, dive in, or jump out.

Psychic pain is a compass for what you need to do.

The thing you've been avoiding is the thing you must do.

The future is always being written. And the author is always the same.
The present.

Socrates said the unexamined life is not worth living. But the overexamined living is not even living.

A mistake can't kill you. But not making them can. Similarly, one mistake can't kill you, but the same mistake a thousand times can.

Learning is action with meditation afterwards.

The stone on your path can block you or it can elevate you

to a higher path. A stepping---stone. It is a matter of choice.

If you are depressed, don't run from it. Embrace it and use it. Point it at something...a book, a painting, a song. You would be in great company.

Mood swings are like weather. Unpredictable and best dealt with by drinking hot tea and great conversation (or great sex).

Life is like a recipe, if you follow the steps in the right order you end up with something delicious. If you follow the steps in the wrong order you end up with a big fat mess.

Successful action is like playing a great guitar solo, you have to play the right notes at the right time with the right intensity. The only way to figure out the right sequence is to eliminate all the bad sequences. In other words, practice till your fingers bleed.

It takes years of training to think logically and abstractly. These people are called mathematicians. If you want to be one treat it like any other profession. Practice by doing. (The best plumbers didn't spend their time reading books about the great plumbers.) Apprentice under a master. (Beginning plumbers don't work alone.) And never give up. (If the first flooded bathroom stopped anyone, then the world wouldn't have any functioning bathrooms).

Left to its own devices the mind will entertain itself, stories of the past, hopes for the future, on and on. But this is not what the mind is for. The mind is a tool. It should work toward an end, preferably one that makes you rich or happy or both.

Just like not everything you do is right, not everything you think is true. The easiest person to fool is you.

If you don't want to have a boss, then you must be one because the price of freedom is discipline.

Procrastination is patience about the wrong things.

Prayer was how your great-great-great grandparents meditated.

Atheists are religious, after all most of them ritually attend yoga, meditation retreats, and functional fitness seminars. If that's not religion I don't know what is. The problem is they took out the best part, God.

Real fear is for running from lions. Modern fear is running from your dreams. Real courage is sacrificing yourself for your tribe. Modern courage is starting a company for yourself. Real love is staying with the same woman for 50 years. Modern love is swiping right on a pale blue screen.

The old kings went out on their great shields, the new ones go out on their gulf streams.

Hard work used to be building bridges and towers. Now hard work is building data bridges and server towers.

Foreign policy experts are like bodybuilders in football pads, they look the part, but they can't run, catch, or tackle to save their lives.

Bleeding heart liberals want to save you, whether you like it or not, you racist fascist son-of-a-bitch!

Politicians are the kids from high school who cajoled the teacher into giving them A's.

Politicians are the talkers not the walkers of life.

Politicians usually have great memory because they have a lot of lies to remember.

A good lawyer can save an innocent man.

A great lawyer can save a guilty one.

Bureaucrats are well-intentioned well-dressed idiots.

Bureaucracy is shorthand for paper shuffling.

Most bureaucrats hate business because they cannot do it.

Most businessmen hate bureaucrats because they cannot stand it.

Some of the best thinkers and writers have been bureaucrats because mundane tasks let the subconscious flow.

Great men combine a great vision with a great work ethic to create great works.

Modern media promotes success as an event, but it's actually a process.

We are all children in God eyes. Therefore, all we do is play, especially work.

If you can see work as play, then you can engage all the best parts of your brain.

If you see work as pain, then you engage all the worst parts of you.

Easy money is like an easy woman. You should be very skeptical.

The harder you have to work for something, the more valuable it is.

Life will only be disappointing if you give up. If you never give up, you never lose. Internally you'll feel like a winner.

I've never met a great golfer who wasn't also good at making money. But I've met many terrible golfers great at making money.

Someone's friends tell you everything you need to know about a person. If they are ugly then the person thinks they are ugly. If they're losers, then the person thinks they are a loser. If they are fun and outgoing, then they see themselves similarly. And on and on.

Some people are born lucky. Others make their own luck. If you're lucky both apply.

Long hair on a woman is beautiful. On a man it is vanity.

Tattoos used to exchange short-term pain for lifelong shame.

The degeneration of a civilization starts with the destruction of the family.

The masters of the universe are the masters of money.

If you want to know who's in charge find out who you can't talk shit about.

Most men live like dogs. Day to day. Following their appetites. Making no plans for the future.

If you want to get something done, then don't do anything except that something.
If you want to run in circles, then don't listen to the line above.

One bummerino can deflate an entire party.

Women today are addicted to their smartphones because it's gossip on-demand.
Men today are addicted to their smartphones because it's women on-demand.
People today are miserable because their addicted to a two-dimensional pixelated version of reality.

Wasting time feels good because it's easy.
Wasting a life feels bad because it's non-refundable.
Wasting anything except your enemies feels bad.

If you apply compound interest to your life, sooner than not you'll be able to have anything you want.

Everyone is insecure.

Bodybuilders are insecure about their body.

Businessmen are insecure about money.

Monks are insecure about life.

Comedians are insecure about fitting in.

Drug addicts are insecure about their thoughts.

Mothers are insecure about their sons.

Fathers are insecure about their daughters.

Women are insecure about their intelligence.

Men are insecure about women.

Aphorisms are only as true as the person reading them thinks they are.

A life well-lived are days lived well. A day well-lived is a decision well-done.

Too much of a good thing is bad. Yet too little of a bad thing is good.

You need hunters to philosophize but you don't need philosophers to hunt.

Some activities are optional. Other are mandatory.

When people sit down to eat or talk but put their phones on the table first they are signaling a lack of presence.

Being present at all times is the highest ideal and the hardest.

Extreme statements are subject to extreme variation.

Life without love is like pizza without cheese.

Words without action are like workouts without sweat.

Nowadays people walk around with their heads down. They are not sad, they are just pathetic. They are looking at their phones. Pay attention idiots!

People with an axe to grind usually don't know how to use an axe.

If running is your only form of exercise, then you are missing the point of exercise.

Men wearing Hawaiian shirts when they are not on vacation makes about as much sense as skiing in July.

Social media selfies are for women. Men who take them are playing the wrong game.

People that wear the same outfit everyday are either geniuses or insane. Either way, they are in rarified company.

Great cooks are fat. Good cooks are ugly. And bad cooks are women who work too much.

Single mothers are either suffering from bad luck or bad decisions, usually both.

Men raised without brothers seek them out in their friendships. Women raised without sisters seek them out in their friendships.

The rise of autism is a troubling and damaging phenomenon. An entire generation of men has been rendered economically useless and emotionally childlike. In Sparta they would have been fed to the wolves. In America they are fed fruit loops. Whoever is behind the epidemic should be forced to hang by their own petards.

Women today are told to be more like men. And men today are told to be more like women. The end result is misery for all.

Women have been pushed into the workforce in order to drive wages down and disintegrate the family. Maybe these weren't the aims, but they are certainly the outcomes.

Women are happiest when they are with their children.

If you want to know how filthy Hollywood is watch how hard the Chinese block its content.

My uncle says Jews are not necessarily smarter than other races, they just help each other far beyond the other races. Compared to the Jewish people, other races act like crabs in a bucket, the higher one goes the harder the others try to pull him down.

If someone calls you a racist while arguing, it's the equivalent to tapping out during a jiu-jitsu match.

Marijuana is the most dangerous drug in the world because it fools you into believing your own bullshit.

Believing is relieving.

Indecision is like a plane taxing on a runaway, frustrating for all involved.

Most women should not be managers because most women are indecisive and afraid of up-front confrontation.

Most men should not be nurses because they lack the empathy and compassion of the average woman.

Homosexuality is not new, the Greeks, the Romans, they had it too. It's typically a signal of decay—not progress.

Working at the ACLU should be a disqualifying experience to serving on the Supreme Court of the United States.

A good joke can melt the coldest heart. A great joke can turn an enemy into a friend.

Coffee works best on an empty stomach.

Happiness is relieving oneself in the woods.

The best real estate is on national park grounds.

Working smart is better than working hard. But the only way to learn the former is to do the latter.

Childlike men and women like anime and manga because it simplifies social interaction into two-dimensional archetypes where everything is explicitly explained. Wise men and women like aphorisms because they squeeze wisdom into a thought.

A man who lives like a forgotten old man when he is young feels like an old

soul thereafter.

A big ego is like a dog who pisses on a tree and thinks he owns it. Deluded at best. Destructive at worst.

If you want to succeed at anything just devote yourself entirely to it. If you want to fail at anything do the opposite of the above.

Nobody knows why we are here. But we are here, and we might as well make the best of it.

Taking life seriously is like going to a rock concert and responding to work emails the whole time.

Money is great up to a certain point, namely up to the point you do not have to think about money.

A beautiful woman can turn even the most powerful men into lapdogs.

Greatness comes in two flavors: the preordained and the premeditated.

If you believe everything people tell you, you are a fool. If you disbelieve everything people tell you, you are a narcissist. If you believe only what's true and none of what's false, you're a genius.

The mind is a great employee and a terrible manager.

Working in a bureaucracy is liking running in a circle while counting to one hundred.

Drugs can be fun. But the fun never lasts. And most people like to have fun too much.

America is a corporation. The president is the CEO. And you are an employee.

The freest men that ever walked the face of the earth are all dead now.

Our desires can be our disasters. But they can also be our divinity.

The dance of duality is everywhere around you. Do not get upset about it. Just enjoy it.

Running a large company is like being a general of a large army. Endless battles. Momentary glories.

A good laugh is a good life.

Focusing on one thing at the exclusion of all others is a mark of control. And a pathway to mastery.

Focusing on many things at the exclusion of one thing is a mark of impulsiveness. And a pathway to disaster.

Multi-tasking is great if you can be in more than one place

at one time. But for everyone else, one task at a time is plenty good.

To the starving man, even dirt is delicious.

Running from your past is like a dog looking for its thumb. Pointless because your past does not exist.

Falling in love can feel like figuring out the universe. And falling out of love can feel like forgetting what you learned.

The dream is free, the hustle is sold separately.

The biggest impediment to your success is You.

The smallest impediment to your success is other people.

The fastest path to success is the most painful.

If you can be productively alone, you'll be a billionaire in this life or the next.

Fear is over-attachment to a temporary state of existence, namely you're body in the here and now. The only way to let go of fear is to touch that dimension of existence beyond the body. And the best way to that is to meditate on nothing and every-thing.

Nowadays everyone is a drug addict, the drug is just so widespread it goes unnoticed. It doesn't hurt that it's got a shiny big screen.

The difference between loneliness and solitude is silence.

When you're lonely the mind can't shut up about how bad your situation is. When you're solitary the mind can't even be heard above the deafening roar of existence. How small you are to think you're ever alone!

A goal can only be achieved when a Process can be accepted, respected, and perfected.

Discontent is a great motivator.

The beginning of Wisdom is the end of Ignorance.

Being Perceptive means being Receptive to the Universe.

If you want to know how to plan for a goal, here is a simple formula: Figure out all the ways to fail achieving your goal; Think of all the wrong actions; Imagine all the wrong decisions —Then do the Opposite and Avoid all the pitfalls and traps you astutely laid out. Often, success is merely just **not** doing a whole lot of wrong things.

There is a place beyond hunger, a place beyond desire, a place beyond fear, few ever get there but those that do are heard of round' the world.

If you're unlucky sit still for a time; if you're luck is overflowing do as much as you can.

It takes an extraordinary person who can sit still without ticking off the seconds, minutes, hours.

It makes for a very ordinary person who can't sit still for a few seconds, minutes, hours without engaging in different activities.

The will to win is the will to survive.

Competition is fine for beasts. But for human beings consciousness is better.

If you ever feel like the worlds passing you by, it is, after all it's been here longer than you and will be here long after you. Just enjoy it while you can.

If you can burn up your karma, then your destiny is your making.

Only when past and future no longer worry you, will you truly start to be alive.

You may sometimes feel like you don't want to be Here, well, you are Here, so you may as well pass the time doing something you like.

Many have withered, some have wondered, few have worked.

Behind every news headline is someone's agenda.

If you want to know how small you are watch an ant. If you want to know how big you are try talking to one.

An outlaw is the freest kind of man on earth. And also, the most confined.

If you want to catch a cheetah, first catch a gazelle.

Good posture is its own kind of superpower.

If money is your god make money. If love is your god make love. If god is your god be godly.

What is truly transcendent, cannot be expressed in words. But only hinted at.

The best drugs can't be put into a pill. And the best pills aren't even pills (red pill—blue pill).

If you learn to play, you'll sooner or later get your way.

It's hard to write because it's easy not to.

People with big heads have a lot of information but not a lot of knowledge.

If you want proof there's more soy in the food, just look around at all the strapping young lads. Oh! Wait there aren't that many left. Estrogen is great for some, terrible for others I suppose.

Sleepless nights make for sleepy days.
And sleepy days lead to late night lays.
But miss the sun for fun at night and you'll never find your way.

Frustration is energy, use it.

A whole lot of not getting what you want is on the way to

getting what you need.

Deprivation breeds pedestalization (i.e. putting things on a pedestal).

The art of living is a living art.

One way or another you end up dead, so don't be afraid to do anything, to be anything, or to go anywhere—ever!!!

Some people say we live in a simulation. If that's the case who's the guy controlling my character!?!?!?

A LARP is a live action role play on the internet. 1 out of 100 LARP's is real. And that's the scary part.

If you spend too much of your free time on message boards, Internet forums, and social media websites, you might just think the world was going to hell in a handbasket. Truth is, it's still ticking and pretty smoothly last time I checked. Sun comes up every day. Sun goes down every day. The moon in its phases. And human beings in their dazes.

A good rainstorm on a summer afternoon feels more cleansing than confession with a priest.

The devil can give it to you, or God can help you do it.

People who love what they do irrespective of money end up making more than those that don't love what they do. And in the case of exceptions the former is happier.

Everyone borrows money, the smart people don't have to

pay it back. These smart alecks tend to be Wall Street Bankers.

A great biker once told me, "Dress for the slide not the ride."

People who talk a lot of shit tend to be full of it.

Tread carefully around the exceptions.

On a man or a woman, but especially a woman, *a tan is the best kind of makeup.*

Cinch by the inch, hard by the yard. One step at a time will get you a dime. But don't stand around, you'll soon be aground.

A world without honor is a world without heroes is a world more like hell than like heaven.

Patience is simply unequivocal happiness with the present moment.

The irony about backwater places is they tend not to have much water. Maybe that's the point.

You drink from the well nearest to you.

CLOSING REMARKS

In the immortal words of Bugs Bunny, "That's all folks!" I hope you enjoyed my words. I certainly enjoyed writing them, at least for the most part. It's taken me my whole life to accumulate all these little sayings in my head, and I hope they can help you along on your path thru this grand existence. Please check out my other books as I release them. Your support means the world to me. Don't be too offended by any of them, it's all in jest. And if you are offended by any of them, well then you must be a pest!

PEACE, LOVE, AND JOY

-Big Ray

ABOUT THE AUTHOR

Big Ray

Big Ray is an anonymous author publishing definitive accounts across various topics. He was born in the United States. He studied at University. He has had numerous odd jobs and is himself quite odd. He does not want personal fame, but he does want  your money, so please buy all his books multiple times. He assures you it will be a dollar well-spent.

BOOKS IN THIS SERIES

Maximal Wisdom Series

Latin Maxims

Business & Finance Maxims

Fitness And Sports Maxims

BOOKS BY THIS AUTHOR

A Rider In The Night

Children Of Helix

Cocaine Daze

Demise Of The West

Eagle And The Dragon

Economics For The Everyman

Gainful Employment

Gospel Of Q

Handful Of Redpills

How To Be: Renaissance Man

How To Do: Bomb Your Driver

How To Do: Microdose Lsd & Mushrooms

Off The Road

S&P 500 Handbook

Scamdemic: Common Sense In Uncommon Times

The Art Of Testosterone

The Beach Party

The Caddy Shag

The Philosopher King

The Weather Warriors

MILLENNIAL MAXIMS